Heads up Lookers and Communicators

Stage 1
0-8 months

Heads Up Lookers and Communicators

ISBN 1-905019-50-5

© Featherstone Education Ltd, 2006
Text © Clare Beswick and Sally Featherstone, 2006
Illustrations © Martha Hardy, 2005
Series Editor, Sally Featherstone

First published in the UK, January 2006

Published in the United Kingdom by
Featherstone Education Ltd
44 - 46 High Street
Husbands Bosworth
Leicestershire
LE17 6LP

**'Little Baby Books'
is a trade mark of
Featherstone
Education Ltd**

Printed in Malta on paper produced in the European Union from managed, sustainable forests

Heads up Lookers and Communicators

Birth to
Three
Matters

Stage 1

Written by Clare Beswick and Sally Featherstone

Illustrated by Martha Hardy

A *Little Baby Book*
Published by Featherstone Education

Featherstone
Education

The Aspects and Components

About Little Baby Books

A Strong Child

Me, myself and I
A sense of belonging
Being acknowledged & affirmed
Developing self assurance

A Skilful Communicator

Being together
Finding a voice
Listening & responding
Making meaning

A Competent Learner

Being imaginative
Being creative
Making Connections
Representing

A Healthy Child

Growing and developing
Keeping safe
Making healthy choices
Emotional wellbeing

Birth to Three Matters (DfES SureStart 2002) the Framework for Effective Practice with Babies and Very Young Children, sends a clear and unequivocal message underlining the importance of home and family working together with practitioners to lay the best possible foundations for life and learning. The Guidance recognises and celebrates the individuality of babies and young children, providing a wealth of guidance and support to those with responsibility for their care and education.

The first series of Little Baby Books was published in 2003 to build on the principles of the guidance and provide practical handbooks, with a collection of easy-to-follow ideas and activities for babies and young children from birth to three. The first series has been expanded to sixteen books, each linked and colour coded to one of the aspects of the Framework, and each offering activities for each of the developmental stages.

These four aspects of the Framework are:
* A Strong Child (Purple Books)   * A Skilful Communicator (Pink Books)
* A Competent Learner (Green Books)   * A Healthy Child (Blue Books)

All the activities in the Baby Books use objects and resources readily available in homes and settings. They allow babies and children to develop at their own pace, to make unhurried discoveries and allow for much repetition as well as trying out of new ideas. This encourages babies to become increasingly independent, making their own choices. All the activities require the careful and skilful support of an adult. The role of the adult is included in the step-by-step 'What you do' section.

Stages of Development

<u>Birth to Three Matters (DfES SureStart 2002) the Framework</u>, uses 'headings to describe children at four developmental stages'. These headings describe children at differing stages of development, linked to broad bands of age.

Young babies from birth to 8 months - **described as** 'Heads up Lookers and Communicators'
Babies from 8 to 18 months - **described as** 'Sitters, Standers and Explorers'
Young children from 18 to 24 months - **described as** 'Movers, Shakers and Players'
Children from 24 to 36 months - **described as** 'Walkers, Talkers and Pretenders'.

Practitioners are encouraged to look carefully at the babies and children in their groups and decide which heading describes these children best. Observations of the children you work with may mean that you refer to the activities for children at an earlier or later stage. This may apply to a whole range of children, including:

babies and children with special or additional needs
babies and children whose home language is not English
babies and children whose development is delayed or more advanced
babies and children who need more experience in a particular component or aspect
children who are new to your setting and need confidence while settling in.

These four new Baby Book collections have been published at the request of practitioners and settings, so the activities can be available in each room. We suggest that you may wish to use the two most relevant books in each room, as this will probably match the broad range of development you work with. However, we also advise you to refer to the whole series when planning experiences for children whose development is delayed or more advanced.

young babies
0-8 months
Heads up lookers and communicators

babies
8-18 months
Sitters, standers and explorers

young children
18-24 months
Movers, shakers and players

children
24-36 months
Walkers, talkers and pretenders

The New Series

Heads up Lookers and communicators

Stage 1

Sitters, Standers and Explorers

Stage 2

Movers, Shakers and Players

Stage 3

Walkers, Talkers and Pretenders

Stage 4

The Little Baby Books in Stages

These New Baby Books are a reorganisation of the material in the original series of 16 Baby Books. They have just been divided in a different way!

Sixteen books have become four books, organised by developmental stage:

This book →

Stage 1   Heads up Lookers and Communicators (Young Babies 0 to 8 months)
Stage 2   Sitters, Standers and Explorers (Babies 8 to 18 months)
Stage 3   Movers, Shakers and Players (Young Children 18 to 24 months)
Stage 4   Walkers, Talkers and Pretenders (Children 24 to 36 months).

Each book contains the activities for each developmental stage, with sections for each aspect and each component. It is for practitioners to decide which stage best meets the needs of the children in their care, and whether to use these books, presented by developmental stage or the original set of sixteen which are presented by Aspect and Component.

The experiences suggested in this book will help young children to grow and develop through a range of planned and informal activities, many of which will be familiar to you. The activities use objects and resources easily available in most homes and settings, they focus on practical activities and purposeful play for individuals, pairs and very small groups. They will help young babies to develop positive relationships and trust as they play and learn with adults and other children.

Each activity page gives step-by-step instructions, tips, plenty of further ideas for children ready for more, practical ideas on differentiation for young babies with special needs, as well as tips on what to look and listen for.

With ideas for home links, These Little Baby Books in Stages continue to give practical support to ensure parents and practitioners are working together to nurture the development and wellbeing of young babies.

Watch, listen, reflect

Assessing young children's learning is a difficult process, but we do know that any assessment must be based on careful observation of children in action. On each activity page, you will see a box labelled Watch, listen, reflect. This box contains suggestions of what you might look and listen for as you work and play with young babies. Much of the time you will watch, listen and <u>remember</u>, using your knowledge of early years and of the children to reflect on the progress of the individual child. These informal observations will help you to plan the next day's or week's activities.

However, sometimes, what you see is new evidence - something you have never seen the baby do before, or something which concerns you. In these cases you might make a written note of the achievement or concern you experience, with the date and time you observed it. You can use these notes for a range of different purposes:

- 👁 to remind you of the event or achievement (it's easy to forget in a busy setting!)
- 👁 to use in discussion with your manager or other practitioners
- 👁 to contribute to the child's profile or record
- 👁 to discuss with parents
- 👁 to help with identifying or supporting additional needs
- 👁 to help with planning for individuals and groups
- 👁 to make sure you tell everyone about the child's achievements.

Observation is a crucial part of the complex job you do, and time spent observing and listening to children is never wasted.

Your role as practitioner or parent will be varied and will include:

* Facilitating	* Observing	* Prompting	* Negotiating
* Supporting	* Imitating	* Celebrating	* Acknowledging

Keeping safe

Safety must be the top priority when working with any baby or young child, in your setting or at home. All the activities in Little Baby Books are suitable for under threes. You will already have a health and safety policy but here are just a few tips for safe play with babies and young children.

Watch for choking hazards

Young babies and children naturally explore toys by bringing them to their mouths. This is fine, but always check that toys are clean. If you are concerned, buy a choke measure from a high street baby shop.

Never leave babies or young children unattended

They are naturally inquisitive and this needs to be encouraged, BUT they need you to watch out for them. Make sure you are always there.

Check for sharp edges

Some everyday objects or wooden toys can splinter. Check all toys and equipment regularly. Don't leave this to chance – make a rota.

Ribbons and string

Mobiles and toys tied to baby gyms are great to encourage looking and reaching, but do check regularly that they are fastened securely. Ribbons and string are fascinating for babies and children of all ages – but they can be a choking hazard.

Clean spaces

Babies are natural explorers. They need clean floors. Store outdoor shoes away from the under-threes area.

Sitters and standers

Make sure of a soft landing for babies and young children just getting there with sitting and standing balance. Put a pillow behind babies who are just starting to sit. Keep the area clear of hard objects, such as wooden bricks. Look out for trip hazards for crawlers and walkers.

Make sure babies and young children are fastened securely into high chairs and that chairs are moved out of the way when not in use. Use a low chair and table for young children. Try to make a foot-rest if their feet don't reach the ground. Watch out for chairs that tip easily.

Contents

About Little Baby Books   page   2
Introduction to this book   pages   3 and 4
Observing and assessing learning   page   5
Keeping safe   page   6

Activities for A Strong Child
Look at Me, Look at You – First contacts   pages   14 and 15
Early Faces – Patterns of faces   pages   16 and 17
Hide and Find – Peep-bo, find me   pages   18 and 19
Look at Me – Mirrors and shiny objects   pages   20 and 21
Rock Stars – Rocking and feeling safe   pages   22 and 23
Look Here! – Imitating facial expressions   pages   24 and 25
Reach Out – Reaching and touching   pages   26 and 27
Take This – Taking hold   pages   28 and 29
Shake It! – Shaking and rattling   pages   30 and 31
Snuggle Up – Feeling close, Feeling good   pages   32 and 33
Hip Hop, Hello Bop! – Rocking and dancing greeting   pages   34 and 35
Time to Go – Saying goodbye at the end of the session   pages   36 and 37
Resources for A Strong Child   pages   38 and 39

Activities for A skilful Communicator
Hello! – Looking, smiling, turning to name   pages   42 and 43
Again! Again! – Asking for more   pages   44 and 45
Peek-a-Boo – Smiles and surprises   pages   46 and 47
Up and Down – Lifting and vocalising   pages   48 and 49
Baby Echo – Copying sounds and expressions   pages   50 and 51
Googoo – Exchanging sounds and noises   pages   52 and 53

Contents

Contents

Copy Cat! – Copying facial expressions	pages	54	and	55
Fingers and Toes – Finger puppet fun	pages	56	and	57
Baby Dance – Moving to a rhythm together	pages	58	and	58
Eye to Eye – Singing and rocking	pages	60	and	61
Here Comes Teddy – Peep-bo fun	pages	62	and	63
Which One? – First choices	pages	64	and	65
Resources for a Skilful Communicator	pages	66	and	67
Activities for A Competent Learner				
Feely Stuff – Exploring fabrics	pages	70	and	71
What's Around? – Exploring the environment	pages	72	and	73
On a Line – Washing lines of things to feel	pages	74	and	75
Spots and Stripes – Patterns and textures	pages	76	and	77
Shake it, Pull it – Strings and ribbons	pages	78	and	79
Squeeze and Prod – Making changes	pages	80	and	81
All Steamed Up! – First marks	pages	82	and	83
Bubbles! – Patting bubbles in surfaces	pages	84	and	85
Hold it – Touching and exploring objects	pages	86	and	87
Tummy Time – A soothing look at mobiles	pages	88	and	89
Shiver and Shake! – Exploring vibration	pages	90	and	91
Pumpkin Pie – Truly messy play	pages	92	and	93
Resources for A Competent Learner	pages	94	and	95
Activities for A Healthy Child				
Reach it – Black and white patterns	pages	98	and	99
Pat it! – Texture and treasure	pages	100	and	101
Grab it – Sticks and shakers	pages	102	and	104

Contents

Peepo – Disappear and re-appear   pages   104 and 105
Look at Me! – A face to face game   pages   106 and 107
Cuddle! – Feeling safe   pages   108 and 109
Happy Hands – Hands together and to face   pages   110 and 111
Look and Pat – Black and white pat mats   pages   112 and 113
Blanket Rockers – Making first choices   pages   114 and 115
Feeling Good – Baby massage   pages   116 and 117
Gently, Gently – Rock and sing   pages   118 and 119
Up the Arm and Down the Arm- A singing game   pages   120 and 121
Resources for A Competent Learner   pages   122 and 123

Aspect and
components

Section 1

The Following section contains activities for young babies, to help build **A Strong Child**

The relevant Birth to Three Matters components are:
* **Me, Myself and I**
* **A Sense of Belonging**
* **Being Acknowledged and Affirmed**
* **Developing Self-assurance**

Heads up
Lookers &
Commun-
icators

Aspect and
components

I like you - you like me

Self awareness, identity

Heads up lookers and communicators

Aspect:
A Strong Child
Components:
Me, myself and I
A sense of belonging

14

Look at Me, Look at You -
first contacts

What you need
* no special equipment

What you do
1. Sit holding the baby in your lap, facing you. Rest your arms on a cushion if you need to.
2. Make sure your face is near enough for the baby to see you clearly.
3. Talk gently or sing to the baby, watching their face all the time.
4. As you talk, sometimes, open your mouth wide or stick your tongue out a bit. Watch to see if the baby copies your expression.
5. Move your face from side to side and watch the baby follow you with their eyes.
6. Keep talking, singing, smiling.

another idea:
* Try the same activity with a hat or pair of glasses on.

Ready for more?
- Make movements with your lips and mouth. See if the baby copies you.
- Do the same activity close to a mirror so you can both see both of you.

Individual needs

☼ Sit or stand with the light behind the baby, not in their eyes.

☼ Make expressions and changes in your face slowly, and hold them for a while.

☼ Give them plenty of time to explore your face with their eyes, and to respond to your expressions.

Tiny Tip

✳ Young babies focus best on faces and objects held at about 22cm.

Watch, listen, reflect

👁 Watch their responses to different expressions, sounds, movements.

👁 Listen, copy and praise any sounds <u>they</u> make.

👁 Watch how they follow your movements with their head and eyes.

Working together

Parents could:

* talk to you about this activity and do it at home.
* take time to talk to their babies in close proximity.
* tell practitioners about their babies' responses.

Practitioners could:

* make sure they spend time each day talking to the babies.
* give parents information about the development of young babies.

I like you - you like me

Self awareness, identity

What are they learning?

are they
  watching?
  focusing?
  looking?
  moving?
  responding?
  copying?
this leads to
  * smiling
  * babbling

15

Heads up lookers and communicators

Aspect:
A Strong Child
Components:
Me, myself and I
A sense of belonging

Early Faces -
patterns of faces

What you need

* small paper plate or white card
* black marker or crayon
* stick, pencil or wooden spoon for a handle
* tape

What you do

1. Make a simple face puppet, by marking a circle of card (or a small paper plate) with a face pattern. Make the pattern very simple (see page 39).
2. Make sure the baby is securely supported in a baby chair, on a blanket or against a pillow.
3. Hold the face puppet about 20cm from the baby's face.
4. Talk as you move the face slowly and smoothly from side to side. Only move the face a few centimetres each way, and stop if the baby loses their visual grip.
5. If the baby reaches out to the puppet, guide their hand to the face.

another idea:
* Make some more black and white puppets with different shapes and patterns

Ready for more?

🖑 Make another 'face' puppet. Glue this one upside down on the stick. Use both puppet and watch to see which face they respond to.
🖑 Glue a plastic toy (a bath duck, plastic car, small doll) on a stick.

Individual needs

☼ Use the puppet carefully with children with special needs. Keep it still and watch carefully to find the baby's focal length.

☼ Don't make these concentrated sessions too long, or the baby may become over stimulated and tired.

Tiny Tip

✳ Talk gently while you play. The baby will respond to the sound of your voice.

Watch, listen, reflect

👁 Watch their responses to the face patterns on the puppets.

👁 Look for any preferences.

👁 Listen for sounds of response and recognition.

👁 Note any movement of the baby's arms, legs or hands towards the puppets.

Working together

Parents could:

★ borrow or make some puppets of their own to use at home.

★ tell practitioners what they observe.

Practitioners could:

★ explain the importance of focusing on faces for babies' development.

★ offer some puppets or puppet instructions.

★ tell parents what they observe when they play games with the babies.

I like you - you like me

Self awareness, identity

What are they learning?

are they
   focusing?
   following
   movement?
   making sounds?
   responding?
   smiling?
   staring?
this leads to
   * recognising
   * focusing

I like you - you like me

Self awareness, identity

Heads up lookers and communicators

Aspect:
A Strong Child
Components:
Me, myself and I
A sense of belonging

Hide and Find -
peep-bo, find me

What you need
* a piece of fabric, thin enough to almost see through (a net curtain, piece of voile, a chiffon scarf)

What you do
1. Sit with a small baby in your lap facing you or opposite you in a relaxer chair or support.
2. Smile and talk to the baby about the game.
3. Hold the fabric up between you, so your face is hidden. Keep talking or singing.
4. Slowly lower the fabric so you can see each other, saying 'There you are!'
5. Don't go too fast at first, the baby has to understand the concept!
6. Now put the fabric right over your head and slowly pull it of, still talking all the time to retain interest.
7. Stop playing when the baby has had enough.

another idea:
* Play the same game with a plain paper plate on a stick.

Ready for more?
- Try gently putting the fabric over the baby's head and slowly pulling it off. Talk all the time and stop if they become agitated.
- Use more opaque fabrics as the baby gets used to the game.

Individual needs

☼ Watch carefully for agitation.

☼ Continue to use transparent and opaque fabrics until you are sure the child is secure with the game.

☼ Try the game with a large soft toy, covering it up and gradually revealing it.

Safety Tip

✳ Never leave small babies alone with the pieces of fabric - they could get tangled.

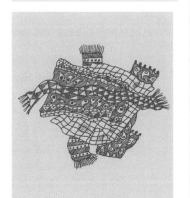

Watch, listen, reflect

👁 Watch to see if they begin to understand the game.

👁 Listen, copy and praise any sounds they make.

👁 Reward smiling, kicking, waving, which all indicate enjoyment.

👁 Note any movement to grab the fabric and remove it from you, themselves or a toy.

Working together

Parents could:

* play this game at home, using a chiffon scarf or sari fabric.
* bring fabrics to use in your setting.

Practitioners could:

* encourage parents to play this game very gently to start with so their babies don't get frightened.
* tell parents about their observations.

I like you - you like me

Self awareness, identity

What are they learning?

are they
   exploring?
   feeling?
   looking?
   grabbing?
   making sounds?
   responding?
   smiling?
this leads to
   * imitating
   * copying

Look at Me

Finding an identity

Heads up lookers and communicators

Aspect:
A Strong Child
Components:
Me, myself and I
A sense of belonging

Look at Me -
mirrors and shiny objects

What you need

* shallow basket or tray
* a baby's safety mirror
* metal serving spoon, pan lid
* shiny and reflective toys and rattles

What you do

1. Clear a space to remove other distractions and make sure the baby is sitting well supported. Place all the shiny objects and the mirror in the basket.
2. Sit opposite the baby and hold the mirror for them to gaze into. Encourage them to reach for and tap the mirror.
3. Share their fascination with the reflection. Sing, 'Look *name*, who can I see? I can see you'. Tap the reflection and then gently stroke the baby's face.
4. Offer them other shiny and reflective toys and rattles to explore. Look for reflections and sing the rhyme again.
5. Allow plenty of time for exploring and repetition.

another idea:
* Get hold of some shiny and reflective paper and fabric, and explore it together.

Ready for more?

* Cover and line a shoe-box with shiny paper and fill with different brightly coloured, shiny and reflective objects.
* Stick some black tape to the mirror to make stripes or concentric circles on the surface.

20

Individual needs

☼ Some babies will need you to take their hand(s) gently to the objects.
☼ Put shiny or bright coloured stickers or tinsel streamers around the edge of the mirror to encourage looking.
☼ Allow plenty of time for babies and children with poor head control to lift their heads to look and focus.

Tiny Tip

❊ Look out for coloured and shiny fabrics in shops selling sari material.

Watch, listen, reflect

👁 Watch how the baby reacts to seeing their reflection. Look at facial expressions, follow their gaze and listen for sounds.
👁 Observe which objects are most appealing to the baby.
👁 Look at the different ways they explore the shiny toys, such as looking, tapping, mouthing and so on.

Working together

Parents could:

* create their own treasure basket of shiny objects at home.
* give their baby a safety mirror to play with at bath time.

Practitioners could:

* suggest items for the parents to use in a treasure basket for their baby to explore at home.
* make a list of all the different ways babies explore objects and look out for these with their key worker children.

Look at me

Finding an identity

What are they learning?

are they
    looking?
    exploring?
    holding?
    grasping?
    making sounds?

this leads to
    * reaching
    * turn taking
    * sense of self

21

Heads up lookers and communicators

Aspect:
A Strong Child

Components:
Me, myself and I
Being acknowledged & affirmed

Rock Stars -
rocking and feeling safe

What you need

* a blanket or square of fleece

What you do

1. Look at the rocking song below. Sing it several times to find a tune and rhythm you are comfortable with. Make the pace slow and steady.

    Rock with me, rock with me, here we go, to and fro
    Rock with me, rock with me, to the stars, and back

2. Now sit on the floor with your knees bent and slightly apart, and your feet firmly on the floor. Hold the baby gently facing you, wrapped snugly in the blanket. Hold the baby so that you can easily gaze into each other's faces.
3. Sing the rhyme, gently rocking together a little way backwards and forwards. Rock to the rhythm of the song, starting and finishing gently.
4. Smile and hold the baby's gaze as you sing and rock.

another idea: Sing the song as you rock the pushchair.

Ready for more?

- Hold a teddy together. Rock the bear from side to side as you sing the rhyme.
- Sit older babies in a large box or plastic crate. Rock it gently from side to side as you sing the song.

Individual needs

- ☼ Give each baby plenty of individual time, attention and encouragement.
- ☼ For babies needing extra reassurance, play the game standing up, holding the baby closely, snuggled in to your shoulder.
- ☼ For babies with motor difficulties, just rock, holding their hands.

Tiny Tip

❋ Pause in the middle of familiar rhymes and wait for the baby to look at you, or make a sound or an action to 'ask' for more.

Watch, listen, reflect

- ◉ Watch to see how the baby is telling you if they like the activity or not. How do they ask you to play the game again? Is it a look, or a sound, an action or body language?
- ◉ Think about how much support the baby needs to maintain their balance as they rock with you.
- ◉ Watch how they are relating to you. Are they enjoying the attention?

Working together

Parents could:

- ✴ try the rocking rhyme at home.
- ✴ make a little rocking session part of every nappy changing routine.

Practitioners could:

- ✴ talk with parents about the importance of rocking rhymes, finger play and knee rides.
- ✴ send home the words and actions of favourite rhymes, enjoyed by the baby at nursery.

Look at me

Finding an identity

What are they learning?

are they
  looking?
  concentrating?
  swaying?
  showing pleasure?
  smiling?
this leads to
  * balance
  * expressing feelings

Look at me

Finding an identity

Heads up lookers and communicators

Aspect:
A Strong Child

Components:
Me, myself and I
Being acknowledged & affirmed

24

Look Here! –
imitating facial expressions

What you need

* floppy hat
* plastic sunglasses

What you do

1. Make sure the baby is sitting well supported. Sit opposite the baby so that your faces are at a similar level. Give them the floppy hat to feel. Hold out an outstretched hand and help the baby to pass you the hat.
2. Pop the hat on your head and sing, 'Where's the hat, where's the hat?' using the tune of the first line of 'Frére Jacques'. When the baby is looking at you, tip the hat suddenly off your head, and say, 'Gone!'
3. Wait to see if they look at or reach for the hat. Play the game again.
4. Try the same game with the sunglasses.

another idea:

* Look out for tinsel wigs and mad sunglasses from fairs and novelty shops. These are great for encouraging looking.

Ready for more?

* Help the baby to gently put the hat on their head. Sing the song and then tip it off gently into their lap!
* Put the hat on a teddy or doll and sing the song.

Individual needs

☼ Some babies may be anxious when your appearance changes. Go gently and keep peeking out from under the glasses or hat so that they can see it is still you!

☼ Help children with motor difficulties to use two hands together.

☼ Look out for glasses with yellow frames a good colour for visual difficulties.

Safety Tip

✳ Ask parents to bring in children's sunglasses and other accessories for exploring and dressing up boxes.

Watch, listen, reflect

👁 Look to see how the baby is asking for the activity to be repeated.

👁 Are they showing surprise and anticipating the hat being tipped?

👁 Listen to the sounds they are using and try to work out what message they are conveying.

Working together

Parents could:

* make this sort of game a part of getting their child dressed.
* hang on to old clothes and accessories to start a dressing up box for their child.

Practitioners could:

* make this game a part of everyday routines in the baby room.
* keep a basket of hats and sunglasses easily accessible so older babies can explore and bring them you to play the game.

Look at me

Finding an identity

What are they learning?

are they
    exploring?
    looking?
    having fun?
    anticipating?
    responding?

this leads to
    * shared
       attention
    * first words

Confidence and competence

Heads up lookers and communicators

Aspect:
A Strong Child
Components:
Developing self assurance

26

Reach Out -
reaching and touching

What you need
* a blanket or cushion

What you do
1. Hold the baby securely so they can see your face.
2. make sure you have the baby's attention.
3. Open your mouth wide and encourage the baby to reach out and touch your face. Praise any movement towards you with their hands or arms.
4. Now put the baby on the blanket or cushion on the floor.
5. Lean over the baby until your face is within reach. Talk to them and encourage them to reach up and touch your face. Remember to give praise and smiles for every effort at reaching, touching, holding.

another idea:
* Hang a small object round your neck and lean over so the baby can reach up for it.

Ready for more?
- Put a light scarf over your head and let the baby pull it off.
- Stand in front of a mirror and let the baby reach out for the reflection.
- Walk round your setting and feel different textures.

Individual needs

✿ Some babies will need you to take their hand(s) gently to your face or an object.

✿ Put a shiny ribbon in your hair or hang a shiny object round your neck.

✿ Allow plenty of time for babies and children with poor head control to lift their heads to look and focus on you.

Tiny Tip

✳ Babies will respond to sounds - use a sound to attract their attention.

Watch, listen, reflect

👁 Watch how the baby reacts to being near your face. Look at their expressions, follow their gaze and listen for sounds.

👁 Watch for favourite sounds or expressions which attract or amuse them.

👁 Watch how they touch, pat and stroke your face or objects.

Working together

Parents could:

* spend a few minutes every day holding their babies and encouraging them to reach out and touch .

* remember to give their babies plenty of praise and smiles.

Practitioners could:

* take some photos of the babies while they are reaching and touching.

* make a list of all the different ways babies explore objects and look out for these with their key worker children.

I can do it

Confidence and competence

What are they learning?

are they
looking?
exploring?
holding?
grasping?
making sounds?
this leads to
* reaching
* turn taking
* sense of self

27

Heads up lookers and communicators

Aspect:
A Strong Child
Components:
Developing self assurance

28

Take This - taking hold

What you need

* a few everyday objects, each small and light enough for the baby to hold and release eg a small whisk, a little wooden spoon or baby spoon, a plastic lid, a little plastic bottle

What you do

1. Clear a space to remove other distractions and make sure the baby is sitting well supported.
2. Sit opposite the baby and hold out one of the objects. Talk to the baby and encourage them to take the object. Hold it close enough for them to take it in their hand, but far enough away so they have to reach out.
3. Let them play with the object, talking to them about it as they do, and giving smiles and praise for holding.
4. Offer them another object (they will probably drop the first one!) and give them praise for taking it.
5. Allow them time with the objects to just play and experiment.

another idea:
* Try some crinkly paper or textured fabric.

Ready for more?

🖐 Make a treasure basket for the babies to play with. Fill it with interesting objects to explore and hold.
🖐 Make a Pat mat from a small zip lock bag filled with cotton wool, crinkly paper or paint!

Individual needs

☼ Make sure the objects are light enough for the child to grip and wave about.

☼ Attach bells or small lengths of ribbon to attract attention.

☼ Give them plenty of time to explore the objects. Sit with them as they do so, giving encouragement and praise for effort.

Tiny Tip

✽ You can get baskets from florists, garden centres and charity shops.

Watch, listen, reflect

👁 Watch for grasping as well as reaching.

👁 Observe which objects are most appealing to the baby.

👁 Change the objects frequently and watch how they respond to new ones.

👁 Listen for vocalisation and sounds.

Working together

Parents could:

★ create their own treasure basket of simple objects at home.

★ give their baby some real things to play with as well as bought toys.

Practitioners could:

★ suggest items for the parents to use in a treasure basket for their baby to explore at home.

★ take some photos of babies playing with everyday objects, so parents understand that play doesn't have to cost money!

I can do it

Confidence and competence

What are they learning?

are they
    looking?
    reaching?
    holding?
    grasping?
    making sounds?
this leads to
    * taking hold
    * selecting
    * sense of self

Confidence and competence

Heads up lookers and communicators

Aspect:

A Strong Child

Components:

Developing self assurance

Shake it! - shaking and rattling

What you need

* some things that rattle - wrist rattles, tins with beads or pasta in, baby rattles, bells, boxes, purses with coins, snack tubes with pebbles, zip lock bags with beads

What you do

1. Collect together a few rattling objects. Make sure they are light enough for the baby to hold and shake.
2. Sit opposite the baby and pick up one of the rattlers. Shake it to attract their attention.
3. Say 'Look. Shake, shake, shake'.
4. Offer them the rattle and wait for them to respond to it. Give it a little shake to tempt them.
5. Try again with another rattler.
6. Allow plenty of time for listening and for the baby to respond. Give plenty of smiles and praise for their efforts.

another idea:

* Try having a rattle each and sharing the shaking.

Ready for more?

- Try rattling under a blanket or cloth and see if the baby can pu the blanket off to get the rattle.
- Try the games with some simple shakers and other simple musical instruments.

Individual needs

- ☼ Give them plenty of time to focus on the rattle and reach out for it.
- ☼ Remember to give praise with your expression as well as your voice.
- ☼ Allow plenty of time for babies and children with poor head control to lift their heads to look and focus.

Tiny Tip

❄ Use glass beads in clear plastic bottles, or coloured water in a leak proof container.

Watch, listen, reflect

- Look at facial expressions, follow their gaze and listen for sounds.
- Observe which rattles are most appealing to the baby.
- Look at the different ways they explore the rattles - banging, shaking, waving. Watch for expressions of pleasure and smiles at your smiles.

Working together

Parents could:

* make some simple shakers at home, using everyday containers and objects.
* spend time playing 'Shake, shake, shake' with their baby, and praising their efforts.

Practitioners could:

* make a display of simple shakers made from everyday objects, to give parents ideas.
* hang rattles over changing tables and mats.

I can do it

Confidence and competence

What are they learning?

are they
- grasping?
- shaking?
- smiling?
- listening?

this leads to
* a sense of success
* a sense of self

Trust,
confidence and
self worth

**Heads up lookers
and communicators**

Aspect:
A Strong Child
Component:
A sense of
belonging

Snuggle Up –
feeling close, feeling good

What you need

* a soft blanket
* baby's own comfort toy
* light and sound musical toy, or
  soothing music and a lamp

What you do

1. Sit with the baby on your lap, so that they can gaze easily
   into your face. Hold the baby's comfort toy within the
   baby's arms and gently lay the blanket over both of you.
2. Sing hello to the baby, stroking their cheek gently as you
   sing their name.
3. Switch on the lamp and music, or light and sound musical
   toy. Place this where it can easily be seen by the baby, at
   their eye level. Tap the light gently to draw attention to
   it, and sing 'Hello baby, hello *name*, hello baby, let's look,
   let's look, let's look.'

another idea:

* Sit with the baby on your knee, facing away from you,
  holding their comfort toy in front of the baby. Make the
  comfort toy dance and then bring to the baby for a hug.

Ready for more?

🖐 Sing good morning to
each baby gazing and
smiling at each other
front of a mirror.

🖐 Play a simple clapping
game and sing 'Good
morning baby, good
morning *name*, good
morning baby, let's jus
say hello'.

Individual needs

- Make sure babies and young children with poor head control are well supported.
- Some babies have difficulty regulating their body temperature. Make sure they don't get too hot under the blanket.
- Use an animated voice to capture the attention of less attentive babies.

Tiny Tip

* Ask parents to bring in a recent baby photo of their child. Cover this with sticky backed plastic and keep it on their high chair, or rest area.

Watch, listen, reflect

- Watch to see if babies are turning or 'stilling' to their name.
- Look to see if the baby is using body language as well as sounds to express interest in the game.
- Are the babies able to anticipate the game as it becomes familiar?
- Are the babies able to relax and nestle into you under the blanket? Do they appear relaxed?

Working together

Parents could:

* add a good night song or rhyme to their baby's bedtime routine.
* snuggle up together with their baby and their baby's comfort toy, to look at a picture book together for just a few minutes every morning.

Practitioners could:

* ask parents to bring their baby over to the key worker to be greeted each morning.
* plan for each key worker to be freed up at the time babies are arriving at the setting to make greeting the baby and parent top priority.

Trust, confidence self worth

What are they learning?

are they
- looking?
- exploring?
- attending?
- feeling comfort?
- making sounds?

this leads to
* sense of self
* feeling of self worth
* self esteem

Trust, confidence and self worth

Heads up lookers and communicators

Aspect:
A Strong Child
Component:
A sense of belonging

Hip Hop, Hello Bop! –
rocking and dancing greeting

What you need
* two wrist toys or pretty hair scrunchies

What you do
1. Slip a wrist toy or hair scrunchy over the baby's wrist and one on your own wrist.
2. Stand holding the baby facing you and close to your body.
3. Sway gently and rhythmically dancing with and smiling at the baby, holding and gently shaking the baby's hand, sing using an animated and lively voice:

   'Good to see you, thanks for coming, hello *name*,
   Good to see you, thanks for coming, hello *name*.'

another idea:
* Sing and dance with other key workers holding babies, with the babies first facing the practitioner, and then facing the other babies.

Ready for more?

🖐 Sit on the floor with the baby facing you, hold their shoulders and rock from side to side. Chant quietly 'Side to side, here we go, stopping now to say hello!'

Individual needs

☼ Make sure babies with physical difficulties feel secure with the movement.

☼ Encourage parents of less confident babies to join in with the song as they hold their own baby.

☼ Choose noisy and bright wrist toys for babies with sensory difficulties.

Tiny Tip

❇ Babies love routine and repetition. Use the same wrist toys each time for this activity.

Watch, listen, reflect

👁 Look for signs that the baby is anticipating the song as the wrist toys are placed over their hands.

👁 Watch to see if the child is expressing feelings about the dance. Are they using body language or sounds to ask for more?

👁 Are the children responding to their name and showing a special bond with their key worker?

Working together

Parents could:

* bring their baby over to the key worker each morning, and join in the good morning routine before passing on other messages.

* talk to the practitioner about how their baby reacts to new places and people.

Practitioners could:

* talk with parents about the value of a routine where their child is greeted and settled in the morning as the parent says goodbye.

* make sure that booklets for new parents contain advice about settling in their baby.

Me and my world

Trust, confidence self worth

What are they learning?

are they
showing pleasure?
enjoying attention?
responding?
this leads to
* shared attention
* confidence
* self esteem
* feeling valued

35

Trust, confidence and self worth

Heads up lookers and communicators

Aspect:
A Strong Child
Component:
A sense of belonging

Time to Go -
saying goodbye at the end of the session

What you need
* special teddy bear
* blanket
* shoe box or toy cot

What you do
1. At the end of the baby's session, give them the teddy to hold and say goodbye to. Stroke the teddy together and tell the baby, 'Time for teddy to sleep' and together put teddy to bed.
2. Keep this teddy special. Encourage the children to hug and look after this teddy.
3. When the baby is going, tell them 'Teddy will see you tomorrow, bye, bye *name*'. Keep this as a consistent routine and a clear end-of-session signal.

another idea:
* Stand with the parent holding the baby, and stroke the baby's hand singing 'Bye, bye *name*, bye bye *name*, time to go go, bye bye *name*'.

Ready for more?
* Give the baby a small blanket to put on the teddy in his bed.
* Encourage the baby to fetch 'special Ted', before saying goodbye and putting it in the cot
* Encourage the baby to pass the teddy to another child.

Individual needs

☼ Look out for a bright yellow teddy with a squeaker for babies and children with visual difficulties.

☼ A soft beanie type teddy will be easier for babies and children with very small hands or fine motor difficulties to hold.

☼ Help babies uncurl their hands by rubbing gently on the back of their hands.

Tiny Tip

✽ Keep this soft toy special. Make him special for all the babies in the room. Introduce Ted to all new parents and their children.

Watch, listen, reflect

👁 Look to see if the child is anticipating the routine. Do they reach for the bear when offered?

👁 Listen to the range of sounds and look for body language that the babies are using to express their feelings.

👁 Does the baby spontaneously hug the bear? Are they able to let go of the bear and let you put it to bed?

Working together

Parents could:

* talk to practitioners about their child's comfort toy and how their child responds to and needs it.

* tell practitioners how their baby responds to preparations for bringing them to the setting.

Practitioners could:

* share with parents every day, some snippet of their child's day, so parents can talk to their baby about their day on the way home, such as 'You had fun splashing the water today'.

* make sure Special Ted is always near at hand.

Me and my world

Trust, confidence self worth

What are they learning?

are they
  learning routine?
  anticipating?
  gaining comfort?
  giving comfort?
this leads to
  * feeling good
  * coping with change in routine
  * pretend play
  * sense of belonging

Resources for all stages of A Strong Child

Puppets

Make simple puppets from:
* old socks
* jumper sleeves
* gloves
* paper plates

Puppets, persona dolls & soft toys

Puppets by Post

www.puppetsbypost.com

Percussion instruments
* IKEA   * ELC
* Mothercare

For cooking & making food (real & pretend)

* plastic plates and beakers (IKEA)

* small plastic jugs

* spoons with chunky handles for serving

* small knives or butter knives for cutting fruit, bread

* plastic or fabric tablecloths

Phones

Use old mobile phones (with batteries removed) or ask phone shops for out of date demonstration models.

Bubbles

Try shaving foam for really good bubbles and for table top fun. Add ready mixed paint for a new experience.

A good value, easy to use desktop digital printer

Hewlett Packard
HP Photosmart 230

Tents and tunnels

Get pop up tents from beach shops

Heuristic Play

More about heuristic play in 'People Under Three' by Elinor Goldschmied and Sonia Jackson

Baskets, containers, weaving materials, dolly pegs

Mindstretchers
Tel: 07768 882537

Scissors for left handers and children with poor grip

ASCO Suppliers
Tel: 0113 2707070

Post boxes, stacking rings, bean bags, threading toys and peg boards, rolling toys, simple instruments and musical rollers from

ASCO Suppliers
Tel: 0113 2707070

Dressing up

Try Charity shops and bargain shops for dressing up clothes, hats, domestic objects.

Cheap clothing

Use fabric remnants and scarves for easy dressing up - fasten them with clothes pegs.

Songs for babies

Rock a Bye Baby
Ride a Cock Horse
Row, Row, Row the Boat
Dance to your Daddy
Bye Baby Bunting
Hush Little Baby Don't you Cry
Down Among the Fishes in the Deep Blue Sea

Some Finger songs and rhymes

This Little Pig Went to Market
Pat-a-Cake, Pat-a- Cake
Round and Round the Garden
She Didn't Dance
Incy Wincy Spider
Tommy Thumb
Five Little Peas
Two Little Dicky Birds
Wind the Bobbin
My Little House
Here are the Lady's Knives & Forks
Here is a Box
One Potato, Two Potato
Peter Hammers with One Hammer
One FInger, One Thumb Keep Moving
Heads, Shoulders, Knees and Toes
Roly, Poly Up and Down
Teddy Bear, Teddy Bear

Dressing up

Try Charity shops and bargain shops for dressing up clothes, hats, domestic objects.

Cheap clothing

Use fabric remnants and scarves for easy dressing up - fasten them with clothes pegs.

Templates for black and white face puppets in Early Faces activity - page 16/17

Heads up
Lookers & Communicators

Aspect and components

40

Section 2

The Following section contains activities for young babies, to help build **A Skilful Communicator**

The relevant Birth to Three Matters components are:
* **Being Together**
* **Finding a Voice**
* **Listening and Responding**
* **Making Meaning**

Heads up
Lookers &
Commun-
icators

Aspect and
components

Heads up lookers and communicators

Aspect:
A Skilful Communicator
Components:
Being together
Communicating
Finding a voice

42

Hello! -
looking, smiling, turning to name

What you need

* teddy bear or other favourite soft toy

What you do

1. Sit opposite the baby or with the baby on your knee. Sit so you can look into each other's faces, at their eye level.
2. Tickle the baby's cheek gently and sing, 'Hello (*baby's name*), hello (*baby's name*), hello, hello, hello'.
3. Take the baby's hand gently to your face and sing the rhyme again, using your name in place of the baby's name.
4. Do this a couple of times, then hold the teddy close to the baby, and help them to hold or pat the teddy. Sing 'Hello teddy, ...'.
5. Give the child plenty of time, attention and smiles. Imitate any sounds they make and encourage them to look at you or the teddy as you sing each part of the rhyme.

another idea:
* Use their own favourite soft toy.

Ready for more?

- Sing the 'Hello song' smiling and waving to the baby in a mirror.
- For older babies and young children, sit together and pass the mirror from child to child, singing the hello song to each child.

Individual needs

☼ Vary the pace or use funny voices and whispers to grab their attention.

☼ Use a soft toy that squeaks when you squeeze it for babies and children that need an extra reward.

☼ Make sure heads are well supported.

Tiny Tip

❋ With parents' permission, display pictures of the babies on the wall and in a book.

Watch, listen, reflect

👁 Watch to see which part of the activity is most rewarding for the baby.

👁 Think about the different ways the baby is communicating, such as facial expression, smiles, reaching, gestures and so on.

👁 Listen to any sounds they make. Are they vowel sounds, consonants, or babble?

Working together

Parents could:

* make the hello song part of the way they greet their baby or child as they wake each morning.
* listen to and copy the sounds their baby is making.

Practitioners could:

* make the hello song a part of the baby's every trip to the changing area or bathroom.
* check that mirrors are at a height where babies can look at their own reflection, as well as share mirror play with staff.

What I really want

Looking, pointing, using sounds & words

What are they learning?

are they
    looking at faces?
    turning to sound?
    enjoying rhymes?
    having fun?
    hugging teddy?
this leads to
    * listening
    * attending
    * turn taking.

43

Looking, pointing,
using sounds & words

**Heads up lookers
and communicators**

Aspect:
A Skilful
Communicator

Components:
Being together
Communicating
Finding a voice

44

Again! Again! -
asking for more

What you need

* bubble pot
* feathers (see tip below)

What you do

1. Sit opposite the baby so that your faces are level.
2. Call their name, then gently blow some bubbles so that they float close to but not into the baby. Say 'Look' and gently reach up and pop the bubbles. Pause for a moment, wait for them to make a sound, reach or gesture to request more.
3. Say 'Again?' then pause. Wait for a sound, word, or gesture, repeat 'Again' and then blow some more bubbles. Give the baby plenty of time to ask for 'Again'.
4. Play the same game with the feathers, blowing them high into the air and waiting for them to float down, before asking 'Again?'.

another idea:
* Play again with squares of tissue or transparent paper.

Ready for more?

* Build towers of bricks. Encourage sounds, words or gesture to mean 'Again', each time the tower is knocked down.
* Play a favourite tickle game and then ask the baby, 'Again?'.

Individual needs

☼ Hold the bubble on the wand and move it slowly in front of babies and children who have visual or physical difficulties. Give them plenty of time to try and reach for the bubble and ask 'Again'.

☼ Use a large bright ball and bounce it in front of children to grab their attention.

Tiny Tip

✳ Craft and needlework shops are great places to find feathers for this activity.

Watch, listen, reflect

👁 Watch their responses to different objects and textures.

👁 Listen, copy and praise any sounds they make.

👁 With older children at this stage of development, listen for sounds and words they use and praise their new vocabulary or copying of the words you use.

Working together

Parents could:

* try some bubble play at home.
* use 'Again' and 'Gone' words and gesture in every day situations, such as bath time and meals.

Practitioners could:

* try different bubble wands to make some huge bubbles, or lots of tiny bubbles.
* talk to parents about the ways babies communicate before words.

What I really want

Looking, pointing, using sounds & words

What are they learning?

are they
  using sounds?
  using gestures?
  making requests?
  reaching?
  looking?
  sharing fun?
this leads to
  * enjoying rhymes
  * exploring
  * making sounds

Looking, pointing,
using sounds & words

**Heads up lookers
and communicators**

Aspect:
A Skilful
Communicator
Components:
Being together
Communicating
Finding a voice

46

Peek-a-Boo -
smiles and surprises

What you need

* squares of net, fur, blanket
* foil survival blanket (from a
  camping shop)

What you do

1. Let the baby pat, pull and explore the fabrics. Feel them
   on yours and the baby's cheek, fingers and toes.
2. Hold out a hand in a 'Give it to me' gesture and say
   'Thank you'. Gently take the fabric, hold it up to your
   face, and play peek-a-boo.
3. Each time you play, let the baby choose the fabric.
4. Spread out some of the survival blanket. Hold it up and
   play peek-a-boo. Hold it high in the air and encourage the
   baby to come under the blanket with you. Snuggle up
   under the blanket, play peek-a-boo with a corner of the
   foil. Encourage eye contact, reward with smiles and lots
   of attention.

another idea:
* Play peek-a-boo round the corner of the door.

Ready for more?

☝ Try hiding noisy toys
under the fabric.
Can you find them
together?
☝ Put the cloth over
dolly's head, play peek-
a-boo. Encourage the
baby to pull the cloth
off dolly on 'Boo'.

Individual needs

☼ Add a rattle or shaker to the 'Peek-a-boo' game for children with visual impairment.

☼ Allow plenty of uninterrupted time and repetition

☼ Try this game with a mirror.

Tiny Tip

✽ Anticipation is an important 'before words' communication skill.

Watch, listen, reflect

👁 Look to see if the baby is anticipating the surprise. How do you know this?

👁 What can you tell from the baby's body language and facial expression?

👁 Watch and listen for sounds and smiles. Reward them with your smiles and sounds.

Working together

Parents could:

* enjoy 'Peek-a-boo' when dressing their baby.
* look out for tickle and action rhyme books at the local library.

Practitioners could:

* make sure parents have information about the ways their baby is communicating.
* give parents plenty of feedback about their child's day, including play and activities as well as information about health, sleep, meals etc.

What I really want

Looking, pointing, using sounds & words

What are they learning?

are they
   anticipating?
   gesturing?
   looking?
   attending?
   choosing?
   having fun?
this leads to
   * first words
   * understanding
   * listening

Making sounds, naming, questioning

Heads up lookers and communicators

Aspect:
A Skilful Communicator

Component:
Finding a voice

Up and Down -
lifting up and vocalising

What you need

* no special equipment

What you do

1. Hold the baby so you are face to face. You could hold them in your arms or under their arms.
2. Look into the baby's eyes and say 'Hello *name*, hello *name*. Shall we play a game?'.
3. Lift the baby up and down gently and say 'Here we go up, up, up. Here we go down, down, down'. Smile as you talk.
4. Do this a couple of times. Use a simple tune or a sing song voice as you talk.
5. Look at the baby all the time, as you play. Imitate any sounds they make and encourage them to look at you as you sing.

another idea:

* Sit the baby in your lap and play the game with a soft toy, lifting it up and down.

Ready for more?

☝ Babies love this game, and some like to be lifted quite vigorously. Play the game standing up, so the feeling of up and down is greater.
☝ Let the baby play the game with a toy.

48

Individual needs

✿ Use whispers or a funny voice to get and maintain their attention.
✿ Play this game gently when an older child is in a hoist or on a changing table.
✿ Support children's heads well when playing physical games.

Tiny Tip

❋ Find toys on strings, springs or elastic and put them where the babies can make them work.

Watch, listen, reflect

👁 Watch for anticipation (wriggles, waving and kicking) as you start this game.
👁 Watch for signs of enjoyment or anxiety as you play - smiles or other expressions.
👁 Listen for any sounds as you play. Older babies may 'sing' with you.

Working together

Parents could:

* make the up and down song part of the way they lift their baby from their cot each morning.
* listen to and copy the sounds their baby is making.

Practitioners could:

* make the song a part of daily greeting as the baby arrives at your setting.
* encourage parents to watch for signs of expectation or anxiety during this game. Some parents can get a bit over-enthusiastic!

What's that?

Making sounds, naming, questioning

What are they learning?

are they
looking at faces?
turning to sound?
enjoying games?
having fun?
showing anticipation?

this leads to
* listening
* attending
* turn taking

Making sounds,
naming, questioning

**Heads up lookers
and communicators**

Aspect:
A Skilful
Communicator

Component:
Finding a voice

Baby Echo -
copying sounds and expressions

What you need
* no special equipment

What you do
1. Sit with the baby in your lap, so your faces are level. When playing with very young babies, keep your face near (about 22cm or 9 inches is the best).
2. Call the baby's name or talk to them to get their attention.
3. Use exaggerated expressions and a lively voice to maintain their interest.
4. Now use a variety of facial expressions and sounds to encourage the baby to watch and copy you. You could try slowly poking your tongue out, opening your mouth wide, 'popping' your lips, blowing out your cheeks, etc.
5. Be patient. Small babies have to work hard at copying you - their muscles are immature. Praise any response!

another idea:
* Play this game at changing time.

Ready for more?
✋ With older babies make the expressions more complicated. Give them time to respond, and praise when they do.
✋ Play the game in a mirror so the baby can see themselves and you.

Individual needs

☼ Give extra time for response, some babies and children may need several seconds (or longer) to 'get it together' to respond.

☼ Play the game with babies in buggies or other chairs – it's a quick way to make contact during the day.

Tiny Tip

✲ Make some simple face masks with paper plates on short sticks to play another game.

Watch, listen, reflect

◉ Watch their responses to your expressions and sounds.

◉ Watch for those babies who take a long time to respond, and give them more time.

◉ Listen for older babies making sounds and responding with words as well as expressions.

Working together

Parents could:

* play this game at home to encourage copying and responding.
* tell practitioners how their babies are responding when they play the game at home.

Practitioners could:

* explain that this game helps babies to learn about turn taking in conversation.
* tell parents about their children's responses to the game, the sounds and expressions they make.

What's that?

Making sounds, naming, questioning

What are they learning?

are they
  using sounds?
  using expressions?
  watching?
  copying?
  concentrating?

this leads to
  * taking turns
  * copying sounds
  * making sounds

51

Making sounds, naming, questioning

Heads up lookers and communicators

Aspect:
A Skilful Communicator

Component:
Finding a voice

Googoo -
exchanging sounds and noises

What you need
* no special equipment

What you do

1. Sit with the baby in your lap, facing you and near enough to see your face.
2. Call the baby's name to attract their attention.
3. Now make a short repetitive sound - 'googoo', 'mama', 'dada', 'lala', 'nana', etc.
4. Wait for the baby to respond. If they don't, make the sound again and wait for a response. Praise any response they make, even if it isn't the same sound as you made!
5. Keep going, taking turns, exchanging smiles as well as sounds.
6. Stop when they lose concentration or interest.

another idea:
* Let them start the exchange and copy their sounds for a change.

Ready for more?

🖐 Older babies and children love echo games. Try some simple 'My turn, your turn' songs or rhymes.
🖐 Try passing an object as you make the sound, eg. a small soft toy, rattle.

Individual needs

☼ Stay close with older babies and children with visual impairment.

☼ Allow plenty of time for them to respond - it may take several seconds (or even longer).

☼ Use a rattle, puppet or soft toy to attract attention in this exchange game.

Tiny Tip

✳ A distance of about 22cm or 9 inches is the best for face to face work with young babies

Watch, listen, reflect

👁 Watch for concentration and whether the baby focuses on your face, mouth and eyes.

👁 Can you tell if the baby is enjoying the game? What are the signs?

👁 Listen for sounds and how well they can imitate and take turns.

Working together

Parents could:

* parents can play the 'nana', 'googoo', 'dada', 'mama' game in the bath, while changing, and even in the supermarket trolley.

* use the game to encourage children to practise family names and familiar objects.

Practitioners could:

* tell parents about the sounds their babies are making in the setting.

* give parents plenty of feedback about their child's day - in play and activities, as well as giving information about health, sleep, meals, etc.

What's that?

Making sounds, naming, questioning

What are they learning?

are they
    anticipating?
    watching?
    copying?
    vocalising?
    initiating?
    enjoying it?

this leads to
    * first words
    * taking turns
    * concentration

53

**Heads up lookers
and communicators**

Aspect:
A Skilful
Communicator

Component:
Listening and
responding

Copy Cat! –
copying facial expressions

What you need

* a few moments of one to one
  quiet time
* a comfortable place to sit
  with the baby

What you do

1. Hold the baby, with head well supported so that you can gaze into the baby's face with ease.
2. Remember that young babies focus best around 20 to 35 cm. that is 8 to 15 inches. Make sure you are close enough for the baby to be able to see you clearly.
3. Sing hello to the baby. Stroke cheeks and gently engage the baby's attention. Pause and then stick your tongue out! Repeat this every 20 seconds or so. Keep going for about two minutes to give the baby plenty of time to respond by copying your action.

another idea:

* Try some different actions, such as wriggling your nose, smiling and so on. Repeat the action for one to two minutes allowing the baby plenty of time to copy your actions.

Ready for more?

- Use a baby mirror together, gazing at your baby's reflection.
- Play anticipation games, such as 'I'm coming to tickle you'.
- Sing rhymes and songs, patting the rhythm out on their tummy or back

54

Individual needs

☼ Support the baby's head well until full head control is achieved.
☼ Strongly contrasting colours and patterns are best for young children at an early developmental stage.
☼ Allow plenty of time for responses. Prompting while they are thinking may throw them off course!

Tiny Tip

❋ Make the movements slowly and give plenty of time for the baby to respond.

Watch, listen, reflect

◉ Look to see how the baby is focusing and following your eyes.
◉ Think about how they are showing their feelings. Are they pleased when they succeed in copying you?
◉ Think about head control and sitting balance for older babies. Does this affect how they respond to you?
◉ Listen to the sounds the baby is making. How do they respond?

Working together

Parents could:

* fix a small baby mirror to their child's baby gym or mobile.
* try some 'Ready Steady Go' play with their baby.

Practitioners could:

* make a booklet of finger rhymes and action songs you use for parents to borrow for home.
* make sure parents know that young babies focus best at 20 to 35 cm, 8 to 15 inches, and what this means for playing, singing and talking.

Let's listen

Listening to learn & learning to listen

What are they learning?

are they
  looking?
  listening?
  responding?
  copying actions?
  interacting?
this leads to
  * attention and listening skills
  * understanding
  * turn taking

**Heads up lookers
and communicators**

Aspect:
A Skilful
Communicator
Component:
Listening and
responding

Fingers and Toes –
finger puppet fun

What you need

* some bright green fur fabric
* fabric glue or a simple
  sewing kit
* scissors

What you do

1. Make a very simple green caterpillar finger puppet to fit
   your index finger. Use fabric glue or simple stitches to
   fix the sides.
2. Have the baby well supported, so that you can gaze into
   each other's eyes, perhaps sitting sideways on your knee.
3. Try this new finger rhyme, gradually wriggling and creeping
   the finger puppet up the baby's arm into the palm of their
   hand, round and round and then down their arm, tummy,
   legs to their toes.

   Wriggle, wriggle, here I come, caterpillar on my thumb
   Round and round, off he goes, all the way down to my toes

another idea:

* Start the rhyme very slowly and pause before running
  your fingers down to the baby's toes for a gentle tickle.

Ready for more?

🖐 Put the baby's hands
between your own and
rub them gently,
singing 'Rub a dub dub,
rub a dub dub'.
🖐 Lie the baby on their
back, hold their ankles
in the air, and play
'Peek-a-boo' between
their feet.

Individual needs

☼ Some children may prefer a gentle pressure to a very light touch.

☼ Gently rub your fingers across the back of fisted hands to help the child to relax muscles and open their hand.

☼ Stopping in the middle of a rhyme, with an exaggerated pause and gasp is a great attention grabber.

Tiny Tip

✻ Inviting people to make simple finger puppets is a good way to get the others involved in your setting.

Watch, listen, reflect

👁 Watch to see if the baby is anticipating the tickle.

👁 See how the baby lets you know they want the activity repeated.

👁 Think about how they are using sounds, body language, expression and eye contact to ask for more.

👁 Listen to the sounds they are making, and note the timing of them.

Working together

Parents could:

* try some finger puppet fun at home.
* borrow some rhyme and action songs books from the local library.

Practitioners could:

* tell parents which are their baby's favourite songs, within the group.
* talk with parents about the range of ways their baby is making their needs and preferences known.

Let's listen

Listening to learn & learning to listen

What are they learning?

are they
   looking?
   anticipating?
   attending?
   sharing attention?
this leads to
   * attention and listening skills
   * understanding
   * babbling and first words

Listening to learn & learning to listen

Heads up lookers and communicators

Aspect:
A Skilful Communicator

Component:
Listening and responding

Baby Dance -
moving to a rhythm together

What you need

* an adult with each baby
* a warm, comfortable familiar place
  <u>Remember</u> - this is a game for babies with good head control.

What you do

1. Make a circle with each adult standing and holding the baby under their arms, with the babies facing the adults.
2. Move around the circle taking steady side steps and sing together, using a tune you are comfortable with:
   Step and step, 1, 2, 3, step and step, dance with me,
   Step and step, 1, 2, 3, step and stop and look at me!
   On the last line, stop suddenly, swing the babies gently high in the air, hold them there, hold their eye contact for a moment before swinging them gently down again and continuing the dance.

another idea:
* Try this game with the babies facing away from the adults. They will love watching each other.

Ready for more?

* Sit in a circle with an adult supporting each baby on the floor. Pat a large beach ball around the circle.
* Still in the circle, give each baby a large floppy hat. Play a game of tipping the hats off.

Individual needs

☼ Make sure the babies have good head control and enjoy this sort of game.
☼ Play each game with one adult and baby to help confidence and reassurance. Later, bring just one more well-settled baby into the game.
☼ Quicken the pace and make the game livelier for older babies.

Tiny Tip

✱ An exaggerated gasp is a winner when trying to grab the attention of babies and young children.

Watch, listen, reflect

👁 Watch to see if the babies are anticipating the lift in the air.
👁 See if they seek to engage your eye contact and attention when you lift them high in the air.
👁 Are they comfortable moving with you to the rhythm of the dance?
👁 Listen to the range of sounds they use to tell you they like the game.

Working together

Parents could:

* dance and sing together. Babies and children love to share adults' music.
* tell practitioners what sort of music their baby likes at home.

Practitioners could:

* build up a collection of varied music to enjoy with the babies.
* make dancing and enjoying music together a small part of every day.

Let's listen

Listening to learn & learning to listen

What are they learning?

are they
  moving together?
  feeling rhythm?
  sharing fun?
  showing trust?
  anticipating?
this leads to
  * shared attention
  * focusing
  * repetition and imitation

Understanding & being understood

Heads up lookers and communicators

Aspect:
A Skilful
Communicator
Component:
Making meaning

Eye to Eye -
singing and rocking

What you need

* a few moments of one-to-one quiet time
* a comfortable place to sit with the baby

What you do

These are the first conversations that babies have with their carers. Every baby needs plenty of quiet conversations.

1. Hold the baby with their head well supported so that you can gaze into their face with ease, and they can see you.
2. Remember that young babies focus best around 20 to 35 cm. that is 8 to 15 inches. Make sure you are close enough for the baby to be able to see you clearly.
3. Sing a simple nursery rhyme or song as you <u>gently</u> rock backwards and forwards (remember, babies need time to focus and follow).
4. Talk quietly to the baby as you rock. Encourage and praise them as they move their faces, hands and bodies.

another idea: * Look, smile, wait for the baby to smile back. Praise them. Try again, smile again, praise again.

Ready for more?

- Each time you change or feed babies, talk to them and make eye contact.
- Look in mirrors with them.
- Sing plenty of rhymes and songs, looking at them as you sing.

60

Individual needs

- ☼ Support the baby's head well until full head control is achieved.
- ☼ Stand where the light is falling on your face so they can see you easily.
- ☼ Some children will find the rocking soothing, others will respond better if you keep still.

Tiny Tip

❉ Make sure your hair is away from your face, so the baby can see your features.

Watch, listen, reflect

- 👁 Look to see how the baby is focusing and following your eyes.
- 👁 Are they following your movement with their eyes?
- 👁 Are they looking at your features - eyes, mouth, hair?
- 👁 Younger babies will often look at your outline, before they learn to concentrate on your features. Note their stage of looking.

Working together

Parents could:

- ∗ talk to their babies as much as they can.
- ∗ use rocking and singing as a way to show affection and to be together.

Practitioners could:

- ∗ explain to parents that babies may not understand what you say, but you need to go on talking to stimulate their brains.
- ∗ make sure parents know that young babies focus best at 20 to 35cm, 8 to 15 inches.

Get the message

Understanding & being understood

What are they learning?

are they
  watching?
  listening?
  copying?
  showing pleasure?
this leads to
  ∗ attention and listening skills
  ∗ response
  ∗ turn taking
  ∗ conversation

**Heads up lookers
and communicators**

Aspect:
A Skilful
Communicator
Component:
Making meaning

Here Comes Teddy -
peep-bo fun

What you need
* a small soft toy or teddy

What you do

This game is about listening and anticipation, making meaning from the tone of your voice.

1. Prop the baby securely in a baby chair or on a cushion. Make sure young babies have head support.
2. Kneel or sit beside the baby, facing them, so they can see your face and what you are doing.
3. Using a suitably enthusiastic voice, say:
   Here comes (teddy/rabbit), here he comes,
   Up your legs and up your tum!
4. 'Walk' the toy up the baby's legs and tummy as you talk.
5. Praise any response and indication of 'again'.

another idea:
* Make the toy appear from different places such as behind the baby.

Ready for more?
- Play other simple games of anticipation such as 'Round and Round the Garden' or 'I'm coming to tickle you!'
- Play these 'wait for it' games at changing time.

Individual needs

✿ An expressive voice and slightly higher tone will attract children's attention and engage them in the game.
✿ Show the child the toy before you start the game, so they know what to expect.
✿ Sometimes stop in the middle of a song, pause and gasp to grab attention.

Tiny Tip

✸ Make some simple finger puppets from glove fingers, to excite and interest babies.

Watch, listen, reflect

👁 Watch to see if the baby is beginning to anticipate the appearance of the toy.
👁 Watch their body and limb movements, and how they respond to attention and games.
👁 Listen to the sounds they are making, and note how long you need to wait for a response.

Working together

Parents could:

★ play very simple games at home.
★ borrow a book of action rhymes from the library.

Practitioners could:

★ tell parents which are their baby's favourite games at the nursery.
★ encourage parents to wait for responses from their babies and praise them when they come.

Get the message

Understanding & being understood

What are they learning?

are they
  watching?
  making sounds?
  responding?
  showing
  anticipation?
this leads to
  ★ attention and listening skills
  ★ understanding
  ★ first words

Heads up lookers and communicators

Aspect:
A Skilful Communicator
Component:
Making meaning

Which One? – first choices

What you need

* a warm, comfortable familiar place
* a basket of small toys and other objects, easy for the baby to hold

What you do

1. Sit opposite the baby.
2. Pick up two of the toys or objects and hold them where the baby can reach out for them. Say in a sing-song voice: *'Which one would you like to have?*
   Take the one you'd like to have.'
3. Hold the two objects where the baby can see them. Watch for a response to one or the other, and encourage them to take the toy in their hand. Name the objects as you offer them. Talk about what you are doing.
4. Let them play with the object for a while before holding out two more objects. Praise reaching and holding.

another idea:
* Play the game with objects that make a sound, or are brightly coloured.

Ready for more?

🖐 Offer babies choices as soon as they can hold something. Try finger foods, pieces of fabric, small soft toys
🖐 Whenever you are with them, talk about what you are doing, even if they don't respond.

Individual needs

☼ Make sure you have the baby's attention before you offer them objects to choose.
☼ Older children with limited mobility need plenty of choices so they feel a sense of control and partnership.
☼ Use familiar and favourite toys for older children.

Tiny Tip

❋ Look in cookware shops and bargain stores for small safe items for babies to play with.

Watch, listen, reflect

👁 Watch for the baby to make a choice. At first they may choose by looking, then by waving or pointing.
👁 Note how long they maintain their attention in the game.
👁 Are they developing ways of choosing, and beginning to have favourite colours, objects or textures?

Working together

Parents could:

* give their children plenty of opportunities to make simple choices.
* play a simple game with their baby every day.

Practitioners could:

* explain why making choices helps children's language development.
* suggest some simple games for babies.

Get the message

Understanding & being understood

What are they learning?

are they
    watching?
    listening?
    making choices?
    enjoying a game?
this leads to
    * making choices
    * conversations
    * naming things

Resources for all stages of A Skilful Communicato

Resources

toy telephones
cups
beakers
spoons
plate
clothes
pairs of socks
pairs of gloves
small baskets
dolls
dolls' clothes
cot blankets
real/plastic coins
purses and bags
paper plates
garden sticks
feely boxes/bags
tape recorder
camera
small world sets
toy vehicles
rattles
tambourines
shakers and bells

Fabrics for dressing up and games

* Try *Fabricadabra*! fabric packs and lycra squares from Featherstone Education (01858 881213)

Dressing up box list

hats	slippers	waistcoats
jewellery	ballet shoes	aprons
scarves	boots	overalls
gloves	flippers	briefcases
handbags	shirts	saris
purses	trousers	overshirts
sunglasses	shorts	glasses
baby clothes	swimwear	cloaks
shoes	large socks	skirts
wellies	coats	

Anthologies

<u>This Little Puffin</u> compiled by Elizabeth Matterson (Penguin)

<u>Bobby Shaftoe</u> by Sue Nicholls (A&C Black)

<u>Lucy Collins Big Book of Nursery Rhymes</u> illustrated by Lucy Collins (Macmillan)

<u>Okki Tokki Unga, Action Songs for Children</u> chosen by Harrop, Friend and Gadsby (A&C Black)

<u>The Little Book of Nursery Rhymes</u> compiled by Sally Featherstone (Featherstone Education)

Action Songs

Wind the Bobbin
Heads, Shoulders, Knees and Toes
Miss Polly had a Dolly
Row, Row, Row Your Boat
The Wheels on the Bus
In a Cottage in a Wood
Simon Says
I Spy with my Little Eye
I Hear with my Little Ear
Who Stole the Cookies?
Put your Finger in the Air
What's the Time Mr Wolf?

Songs to help imitation & imagination

I'm a Little Teapot
Five Currant Buns
Miss Polly had a Dolly
Row, Row, Row Your Boat
The Wheels on the Bus
Dingle Dangle Scarecrow
Little Peter Rabbit
Here we go Round the Mulberry Bush
There was a Princess Long Ago
In Cottage in a Wood
I Can Play on the Big Bass Drum
I Went to Visit the Farm One Day

Everyday objects

keys
cup
spoon
plate
hat
shoe
car
bus
flannel
brush
toothbrush
sponge
sock
purse
dog
cat
book
telephone
bowl
basket
toy tele-
phones
cups
beakers
spoons
plates
clothes

dolls
dolls'
clothes
cot blankets
plastic coins
purses bags
paper plates
garden
sticks
tape
recorder
camera
toy vehicles
rattles
shakers bells

pairs of
gloves
socks
shoes
trainers
boots
chopsticks
drumsticks
cymbals
shakers

For music and movement

shakers
bells
drums
castanets
rattles
sticks
chime bars
tins
cans
old
saucepans
metal teapots
spoons

tambourines
gloves
cloaks
shoes
ribbons
balloons
lycra squares
and strips
gauze
net
feathers
bubbles
foam

Pictures of objects and people

Collect some pictures of objects and faces (use catalogues, magazines, old books, brochures) and real objects that match. Take some photos of objects in your setting and put them with the real object.
Take some photos of the people in your setting and outside to recognise and name.
Always ask permission before photographing anyone!

Aspect and
components

Section 3

The Following section contains activities for young babies, to help build
A Competent Learner

The relevant Birth to Three Matters components are:
* **Being Imaginative**
* **Being Creative**
* **Making Connections**
* **Representing**

Heads up
Lookers &
Commun-
icators

Aspect and
components

Touch it - feel it

Sensory play through touch

Heads up lookers and communicators

Aspect:
A Competent Learner

Components:
Being imaginative
Being creative

Feely Stuff - exploring fabrics

What you need

* pieces of fabric (if you don't have any, collect some bits of clothing with different textures) - fur, wool, plastic, leather, denim, fleece, cotton, net or a feather!

What you do

Have the fabrics in your lap with the baby.
1. Choose a piece of fabric and put it on the baby's arm, leg, hand, cheek, fingers or toes.
2. Stroke the baby's skin gently with the fabric.
3. Talk about the feel of the fabric, using simple words such as soft, smooth, shiny. Make it into a little sing-song chant if you like.
4. Encourage the baby to hold the fabric with two hands.
5. Try helping the baby to bring the fabric towards their face.
6. Change to a new fabric when they seem ready.

another idea:
* Put the baby on different fabrics when they lie on the floor.

Ready for more?

☝ Help the child to choose a piece of fabric, and feel it on their skin. If the piece is big enough, join in!
☝ Gently put a piece of fabric over the baby's head (and yours). Play Peep-Bo!

Individual needs

☼ Start with one or two textures.
☼ Watch carefully for likes & dislikes.
☼ Stroking on the cheek with fabric or a feather is a very soothing sensation for most babies, and many older children.
☼ Give them plenty of time to explore and enjoy each texture.

Tiny Tip

✽ Try warming the fabric in the tumble drier or on the radiator before use.

Watch, listen, reflect

👁 Watch their responses to different objects and textures.
👁 Listen, copy and praise any sounds they make.
👁 With older children, listen for sounds and words they use and praise their new vocabulary or copying of the words you use.
👁 Listen for comparisons such as 'Like my kitty' or 'Daddy shoes'.

Working together

Parents could:

* bring in snippets of fabrics (eg wedding dress material, saris, fur, embroidery).
* do the activity at home, using describing or comparing words, perhaps when children are undressing for bed.

Practitioners could:

* work with parents to collect a range of fabrics (these will need to be washed and checked frequently).
* check out toy library collections for textured toys and activities.

Touch it - feel it

Sensory play through touch

What are they learning?

are they
   exploring?
   feeling?
   looking?
   sharing?
   making sounds?
   responding?
   smiling?
this leads to
   * imitating
   * comparing

Touch it - feel it

Sensory play through touch

Heads up lookers and communicators

Aspect:
A Competent Learner

Components:
Being imaginative
Being creative

What's Around? - exploring the environment

What you need

* no special equipment, just a good eye for what your setting or home offers
* look around before you start to find places with interesting things to touch and feel

What you do

1. If you are with a young baby, carry them to different parts of the room to feel different things.
2. Point to each object, name it, then pick it up and bring it near to the baby.
3. Talk about the object, what it looks and feels like. Use describing words like 'lumpy', 'smooth', 'shiny'.
4. Encourage the baby to touch or hold it by bringing it nearer.
5. Visit a different part of the room to look at something else. Choose things that feel different - smooth/bumpy, shiny/matt, soft and warm/cold and hard.

another idea:
* If the baby is able to sit, bring objects for them to hold, and sit opposite them to talk about them.

Ready for more?

* Collect some objects in a basket and let them choose.
* Encourage them to point to other objects they want to look at. Bring these to them and praise their communication.

Individual needs

☼ Explore just 2 or 3 things to start with.

☼ Make sure the objects are small enough for babies to see and hold, but not so small they get dropped!

☼ Give children time to feel the objects - don't be in a hurry. One interesting object may hold their attention for some time.

Tiny Tip

✳ Try feeling some fruits and vegetables with textured peels and skins.

Watch, listen, reflect

👁 Watch to see how babies focus - make sure the object isn't too close or too far away.

👁 Watch for and reward every response - reaching, grasping, talking, smiling, looking. Use the words 'Good looking', 'Good smiling' so they know what you like.

👁 Note the time when they start to pass things from hand to hand.

Working together

Parents could:

* play this game at home, it doesn't need any preparation!

* bring interesting objects to your setting - fruit, vegetables, ornaments, fabrics, clothing, souvenirs.

* tell you about things their children like to touch.

Practitioners could:

* check each week to be sure there are new things to look at, smell, feel and touch.

* bring or collect local items which reflect the community and children's lives and interests.

Touch it - feel it

Sensory play through touch

What are they learning?

are they
  exploring?
  feeling?
  looking?
  making sounds?
  responding?
  enjoying your company?
this leads to
  * imitating
  * comparing

Touch it - feel it

Sensory play through touch

Heads up lookers and communicators

Aspect:
A Competent Learner

Components:
Being imaginative
Being creative

74

On a Line -
washing lines of things to feel

What you need
* lots of different surfaces and textures: pieces of fabric, corrugated card, bubble wrap, pegs, a glove, some big beads or buttons. etc.
* string, wool or a long shoe lace

What you do
1. Put the baby in a seat or prop them with a cushion.
2. Make the washing line where the baby can see you.
3. Talk about what you are doing as you make the game, and name the things you are tying on.
4. Using small bits of string or wool, attach some of the things you have collected firmly to a long piece of string or shoe lace (trainer laces are a good length).
5. When you have about six different things fixed on the string, hold it where the baby can see and reach it.
6. Encourage the baby to reach out for the things on the string and pull them towards her. Talk and listen.

another idea:
* Fix the washing line above the changing table, or from side to side of the cot or buggy.

Ready for more?
* Make washing lines with moving pieces threaded on the string.
* Try adding things that make sounds such as bells, shells, rattles, or small toys with different textures.

Individual needs

☼ You may need to guide the baby's hands towards the objects.

☼ Check to make sure they can see the objects.

☼ Find out which textures they seem to like, and talk about these.

☼ Give them plenty of time.

Safety Tip

✳ Make sure everything is securely fixed to the line, and there are no sharp edges.

Watch, listen, reflect

👁 Watch their responses to different textures.

👁 Look at how they begin to move and control their fingers and hands, and how the movements of their legs and arms tell you if they are enjoying the game.

👁 Watch for babies using both hands and feet to reach for objects.

Working together

Parents could:

★ contribute things for the strings.

★ take some of the strings home to share.
Remind parents that they should stay with the baby while they play, so they don't get tangled in the string.

Practitioners could:

★ change the objects on the strings frequently.

★ look for new ideas of things to string.

★ tell parents about the new things their babies can do, that you have observed while playing the game.

Touch it – feel it

Sensory play through touch

What are they learning?

are they
  exploring?
  moving fingers?
  looking?
  sharing?
  making sounds?
  responding?
  reaching?
  concentrating?
this leads to
  * imitating
  * comparing

Count with Me

Pattern, shape & early counting

Heads up lookers and communicators

Aspect:
A Competent Learner

Components:
Making connections

Spots & Stripes -
patterns and textures

What you need

* everyday objects with spots, stripes, slots and holes (eg. tea strainer, draining spoon, spaghetti measurer, biscuit cutters, stripey tea towel)
* a tray

What you do

1. Clear a space and remove other distracting objects.
2. Make sure the baby is sitting in a well supported position.
3. Offer the baby one of the objects. Encourage reaching, grasping and holding with two hands.
4. Explore the object together. Try feeling it on hands or feet. Feel the holes, peep through the slots, touch the spots. Change to a new thing when they are ready.
5. Allow plenty of time to explore the tray of objects without interruption. Stay with them while they explore.

another idea:

* Find lots of wooden objects with holes, stripes, and textures to explore.

Ready for more?

🖐 Try cutting holes and slits in fabric to poke hands through.

🖐 Explore hair scrunchies bangles and bracelets together.

🖐 Provide a collection of card and plastic tubes to explore.

Individual needs

☼ Some babies will need you to take their hand(s) gently to the objects.

☼ Look out for bright or fluorescent colours for visually impaired babies.

☼ Gently tickle the back of the hand to help babies with clenched fists open their hands.

Tiny Tip

❋ Make sure the baby is in a good light when they are exploring.

Watch, listen, reflect

👁 See which patterns and objects are most interesting to the baby.

👁 Watch how the baby explores the objects with their hands and mouth.

👁 Listen and copy any sounds the baby makes. What is the baby trying to communicate with these sounds?

Working together

Parents could:

* bring in everyday objects and fabrics with spots and stripes.
* watch how their baby explores everyday objects.

Practitioners could:

* suggest items for the parents to use in a treasure basket of everyday objects to explore at home.
* make a list of all the different ways babies explore objects and look out for these with their key worker children.

Count with me

Pattern, shape & early counting

What are they learning?

are they
  looking?
  holding?
  exploring?
this leads to
  * grabbing
  * reaching
  * making choices
  * investigating

Heads up lookers and communicators

Aspect:
A Competent Learner

Components:
Making connections

Shake it, Pull it -
strings and ribbons

What you need

* ribbon
* scissors
* plastic bangles
* small shakers, bells and rattles

What you do

1. Cut several pieces of ribbon, about 30cm long.
2. Tie a plastic bangle to each cut length of ribbon. Tie a rattle, shaker or bells to the other end of each ribbon. Check that all is secure.
3. Place one of the shakers on the floor or tray in front of the baby. Offer them the bangle to hold. Help them to grasp it.
4. Talk and sing to the baby as they explore the bangle. Gently tug the ribbon and shaker towards them, and encourage them to try pulling. Reward any attempt to pull by smiling and saying 'again?'

another idea:
* Use a tin tray as a noise maker for this activity.

Ready for more?

* Use different texture of string and ribbon attached to different sound makers.
* Fix a plastic spoon to a ribbon as an alternative type of handle.
* Play the same game lying on tummies.

Individual needs

✿ For babies and toddlers with fine motor difficulties, try a Velcro wristband for one end of the ribbon.

✿ For babies needing extra help, enjoy pulling the bangle and exploring the sound maker together. Choose sound makers that are particularly interesting to that baby or child.

Tiny Tip

❊ Check regularly to make sure all ribbons are secure.

Watch, listen, reflect

👁 Watch to see if the baby is making discoveries accidentally, or exploring more purposefully.

👁 Look to see how they are using all their senses to explore the objects.

👁 Listen to the range of sounds they are making.

Working together

Parents could:

* give their baby time to fiddle with strings and ribbons, eg. labels attached to blankets or soft toys, ribbons and ties on their own clothes.
* try to obtain some board books with textures and ribbons to feel.

Practitioners could:

* talk with parents about how babies explore and investigate as a means of understanding how their world works.
* talk with parents about how the baby is making connections and finding out about objects when they play.

Count with me

Pattern, shape & early counting

What are they learning?

are they
   exploring?
   curious?
   reaching?
   grasping?
   showing pleasure?

this leads to
   * exploring
   * understanding cause & effect

Heads up lookers and communicators

Aspect:
A Competent Learner

Components:
Making connections

Squeeze & Prod -
making changes

What you need

* small quantities of cooked sticky rice, mashed potato, jelly
* small plastic bowls & cups
* small plastic trays, freezer box lids, plant trays etc.

What you do

1. Make sure the baby is sitting well supported in a baby chair and dressed (or undressed!) ready for messy play.
2. Sit opposite the baby and place a small quantity of sticky rice on their tray. Pat it, prod it and then gently squeeze some through your own fingers. Encourage them to feel it.
3. Help them to squeeze it, poke it through your fingers and so on. Cup your hand for them to poke some rice in.
4. Give plenty of uninterrupted time and attention. Encourage the baby to pat and rub the rice with both hands too.
5. Try with the mashed potato and then with the jelly. You could mix them all together for a very messy medley!

another idea:
* Try some very soft bread dough instead.

Ready for more?

🖐 Make small sticky rice balls and hold them ou for the baby to reach for and grasp.
🖐 Add a slotted spoon, o plastic potato masher to pound, mix and poke
🖐 Try rice, jelly and potat in plastic eggcups.

80

Individual needs

☼ Be mindful that some babies and children may be wary of such new textures.
☼ Make sure the tray is at the right height and position for babies or children with motor difficulties.
☼ Give the baby or child extra time – they may prefer to watch you first!

Safety Tip

✳ Vary the amount of material offered. Tiny amounts allow different things to be discovered.

Watch, listen, reflect

👁 Watch how the baby is exploring. Think about the sorts of discoveries they are making as they explore.
👁 Watch and listen to how they express their feelings; maybe you can see excitement, pleasure, or perhaps dislike in their expressions, movements or the sounds they make.

Working together

Parents could:

* try and give their baby time to explore different textures and foods.
* help their baby to squeeze and prod flannels and sponges at bath time.

Practitioners could:

* plan lots of opportunities for exploring and investigating.
* have a box of appropriate foodstuffs ready to hand so this activity can easily and quickly be prepared.

Count with me

Pattern, shape & early counting

What are they learning?

are they
　feeling texture & change?
　exploring things?
　having an effect?
　sharing the experience?

this leads to
* cause & effect
* fine motor control

Heads up lookers and communicators

Aspect:
A Competent Learner
Components:
Representing

All Steamed Up! – first marks

What you need

* a mirror or window

What you do

1. Hold the baby in your arms and stand very near the window or mirror, so you can both see. Talk to the baby all the time as you look at each other in the mirror
2. Gently breathe on the window or mirror, so a small patch of the glass steams up. Say 'Look, all gone!' as you disappear in the steam.
3. Make sure the baby is looking at the steam. Now clear the small patch of steam away with your hand.
4. Greet the baby in the mirror again.
5. Now breathe on a different part of the mirror or window and draw a smiling face in the steam.

another idea:

* Get up really close and let the baby pat the mirror so they make marks too.

Ready for more?

🖐 Use a small hand mirror for the same game.
🖐 Play this game at changing or bath time.
🖐 Provide mirrors on walls at low levels so babies can see themselves as they play.

Individual needs

☼ Some babies will need you to take their hand(s) gently to the mirror to help them concentrate.

☼ Have a light shining on your faces, not behind you, so babies with visual or concentration difficulties can see your faces clearly.

Tiny Tip

❋ Try to reduce distractions behind you which could be reflected in mirrors or windows.

Watch, listen, reflect

👁 Watch the baby's face in the mirror to check if they are focussing on the reflections.

👁 Notice any reaching, and encourage by moving closer.

👁 Listen and copy any sounds the baby makes. What is the baby trying to communicate with these sounds?

Working together

Parents could:

* play this game at bath time.
* hang or suspend a safety mirror over their cot or changing mat.

Practitioners could:

* put safety mirrors in the toy library or loan collection.
* explain the value of early mark making to parents.
* put mirrors at low levels in the setting.

Make your mark

Early marks and writin

What are they learning?

are they
    looking?
    reaching?
    responding?
this leads to
    * using fingers
    * using hands
    * investigating

Heads up lookers and communicators

Aspect:
A Competent Learner
Components:
Representing

84

Bubbles! -
patting bubbles in surfaces

What you need

* bubbles and blower

What you do

1. Make sure the baby is sitting or propped in a well supported position, near a flat surface - a changing table, a wall, a low table, a tray, a baby chair with a table.
2. Sit opposite the baby and gently blow some bubbles towards them, being careful not to blow them in their face!
3. Try to blow the bubbles near their hands, so they can touch and reach for them.
4. Now blow some bubbles so they land on the flat surface. Put your hand out and pat or poke some of the bubbles. Encourage the baby to reach out too and pat the bubbles as they land.

another idea:
* Try blowing bubbles at changing time.

Ready for more?

🖐 Put some very bubbly washing up liquid foam on a tray so they can pat and feel it.
🖐 Give plenty of patting experience with 'pat mats' - small fabric or plastic bags filled with crinkly paper, cooked pasta, rice.

Individual needs

☼ Blow the bubbles in a bright or directed light so the baby can focus on them.
☼ Use bubbles, foam, pat mats etc on wheel chair or buggy trays.
☼ Remember to blow bubbles gently, some babies hate to feel them on their faces or hands.

Tiny Tip

❋ Bubbles are very good for gaining a baby or child's attention, or rewarding them.

Watch, listen, reflect

◉ Watch for reaching and patting, and note how the baby is using their hands.
◉ Listen for any sounds and expressions of pleasure - make sound back!
◉ Watch their concentration and stop the game when they lose interest.

Working together

Parents could:

* play bubble games with their babies at bath or changing times.
* play patting games with bubbles, shaving foam etc.

Practitioners could:

* buy bubbles in bargain pots and refill containers for loan to parents.
* enjoy the simple fun of bubble making indoors and outside.

Make your mark

Early marks and writing

What are they learning?

are they
    watching?
    reaching?
    patting?

this leads to
    * holding
    * concentrating
    * work with fingers
    * investigating

Make your mark

Early marks and writing

Heads up lookers and communicators

Aspect:
A Competent Learner

Components:
Representing

Hold it –
touching and exploring objects

What you need

* pieces of gift ribbon, string or cord
* small objects, such as clean feathers, beads, small bells, teaspoons, hair scrunchies, even screwed up paper!

What you do

1. Cut some lengths of string or ribbon and tie one object on the end of each.
2. Have the baby facing you in a chair or on a rug or mat.
3. Choose one of the strings and dangle the object in front of the baby, just within reach of their outstretched arms.
4. Keep it as still as possible, so the baby can focus on it, but not too close!
5. Talk to the baby and encourage them to reach out for the object. Move the string so the baby can pull the object towards them.
6. Try again with another object string.

another idea:

* Hang strings above the changing area, change the objects every few days.

Ready for more?

* Make a simple mobile and hang it above the babies while they are lying down.
* Hang old CDs in trees and bushes outside and watch them shining when you are in the garden with the babies

Individual needs

☼ Make some object strings to hang from frames and baby gyms.
☼ Some babies will need you to take their hand(s) gently to the objects.
☼ Look for brightly coloured objects and things that make sounds for children with visual difficulties.

Tiny Tip

❋ Put a pillow or cushion each side of a lying down baby to help them keep still and concentrate.

Watch, listen, reflect

👁 Watch for the comfortable focusing distance - it's different for each child.
👁 Note which objects the baby prefers.
👁 Watch how the baby explores the objects with their hands and mouth.
👁 Watch how they use fingers and hands to grab and hold.

Working together

Parents could:

* put a home made mobile above their baby's cot or changing table.
* tell practitioners which objects their baby likes.

Practitioners could:

* have a mobile making workshop with parents. Use wire coat hangers, gift ribbon and simple objects.
* hang plenty of objects up in the setting to give parents ideas they could use at home.

Make your mark

Early marks and writing

What are they learning?

are they
   looking?
   reaching?
   holding?

this leads to
   * grabbing
   * hand control
   * focusing
   * holding

Let's explore

Exploring and creating

Heads up lookers and communicators

Aspect:
A Competent Learner

Component:
Being creative

Tummy Time –
a soothing look at mobiles

What you need

* simple mobiles: black and white, reflective, fluorescent, musical
* a rug for the baby to lie on or a nest of cushions

What you do

1. Make sure the baby is warm and comfortable, lying on the rug. Enclose the space with cushions. Hang mobiles above the baby so they can gaze and focus on them.
2. Remember that young babies focus best around 20 to 35cm; 8 to 15 inches. The mobiles should be close enough for the baby to be able to see clearly. Check that mobiles are fixed securely and that older babies patting them will not become entangled.
3. Tap the mobiles gently and talk to the baby, encouraging them to look towards the mobiles. Hum a gentle tune, encouraging babies to track the mobile from side to side.

another idea:

* Put them on their tummy and roll brightly coloured or noisy toys from side to side for them to focus on.

Ready for more?

🖐 Use glitter sticks, or bubble tubes to encourage looking and reaching
🖐 Shine a torch light on to a white tray for the baby to follow.
🖐 Put brightly coloured windmills by an open window for gazing.

Individual needs

✿ Make sure the baby's head is well supported until full control is achieved.

✿ Black-and-white or contrasting colours and patterns are best.

✿ Experiment by holding the mobiles in different positions to see where children can most easily focus.

Tiny Tip

✳ Roll up two small towels and place one each side of the baby to give them extra support and comfort.

Watch, listen, reflect

👁 Look to see how the baby is focusing on and following objects.

👁 How are they showing their feelings? Which colours and mobiles are most appealing to each baby?

👁 Consider how the baby looks and tracks the mobiles when lying on their back and on their tummy.

👁 Listen to the sounds the baby is making.

Working together

Parents could:

* try different mobiles and toys for looking.
* make sure their baby has plenty of time playing on their tummy as well as on their back.

Practitioners could:

* visit the local toy library for different mobiles.
* make sure parents know that young babies focus best at 20 to 35cm, 8 to 15 inches, and what this means for playing and for singing and talking to their baby.

Let's explore

Exploring and creating

What are they learning?

are they
  looking?
  following?
  responding?
  attending?
this leads to
  * looking and tracking
  * sensory play
  * shared attention and fun

Exploring and
creating

**Heads up lookers
and communicators**

Aspect:
A Competent
Learner
Component:
Being creative

Shiver and Shake! -
exploring vibration

What you need

* massage rollers
* vibrating toys
* balloon
* drum or tambourine

What you do

1. Sit with the baby well supported, so you can gaze easily into each other's faces. Gently tap with your fingertips the baby's hands and lower arms. Sing 'Tap, tap, tap' pause, 'Tap, tap, tap', stop.
2. Next give the baby the massage roller to feel. Help them to hold it in both hands. Feel it on finger tips, palms, backs of hands. Very gently roll it up the baby's forearms.
3. Watch carefully to see how the baby responds to the unfamiliar sensations.
4. Try touching the vibrating toys, and tapping the balloon together, or put the baby's hands on the drum or tambourine as you tap the edges to make it gently vibrate.

another idea:
* Fix ribbons tightly across a tray top. Ping the ribbons.

Safety!
Take great care with balloons, they c[an] be a real chokin[g] hazard!

Ready for more?
* Try the vibrating toys and massage rollers on legs, feet and toes!
* Lie the baby gently over a large exercise ball, or space hopper. Gently tap the sides o[f] the ball and feel the vibrations.

Individual needs

☼ Children with physical difficulties, especially cerebral palsy, are hypersensitive to some sensations. Be watchful and respectful of their responses.

☼ Look for noisy, bright vibrating toys to stimulate children with profound difficulties, who are at a very early developmental stage.

Tiny Tip

✲ Wind-up toys are a great way to encourage looking and reaching. Set them going on tray tops, or metal tin lids for some extra noisy play.

Watch, listen, reflect

👁 Watch how the baby is responding to each new experience. How are they letting you know how they feel?

👁 Listen to the range of sounds they are using.

👁 Look to see if they are sharing their pleasure in the experiences with you.

Working together

Parents could:

* explore musical toys and instruments with their baby.
* make sure their baby has plenty of opportunity to touch and explore a wide range of objects and textures, especially when they are out and about.

Practitioners could:

* make a collection of vibrating toys and massage rollers.
* talk to parents about the importance of sensory play and exploration and share some simple ideas to try at home.

Let's explore

Exploring and creating

What are they learning?

are they
  looking?
  reaching?
  patting?
  grasping?
  exploring?
this leads to
  * shared fun
  * sensory play
  * creating

**Heads up lookers
and communicators**

Aspect:
A Competent
Learner
Component:
Being creative

Pumpkin Pie -
truly messy play!

What you need

* a pumpkin
* a sharp knife and chopping
  board
* a pan and access to a stove
  or hob
* potato masher, milk

1. Peel the pumpkin carefully and chop into even-sized
   chunks. Boil for 25 minutes, drain and mash. Add some
   cold milk and mash to a smooth consistency. Leave until
   cool.
2. Make sure the baby is sitting supported in a chair or on
   your knee. Squeeze the mashed pumpkin through your
   fingers. Give the baby a chance to smell and feel the texture.
3. Encourage the baby to touch your hands and pat at the
   mashed pumpkin. Hold the baby's hands gently in yours,
   and if they are enjoying the experience, rub hands
   together gently exploring the texture of the pumpkin.

another idea:
* Try this with mashed pumpkin straight from the fridge,
  for a very different sensation.

Ready for more?

⚫ Try isolating index fin
  gers and poking them
  deep into the mash.
⚫ Pour a little water ove
  the mash and explore
  the changing textures
⚫ Add a small wooden
  spoon to bash the
  mashed pumpkin!

Individual needs

✿ Set the yellow - orange mash against a black surface for maximum contrast for visually impaired babies.

✿ Some babies and older children really don't like the feel of messy play. Provide some clean handled spoons and plastic brushes for them to explore the mashed pumpkin.

Tiny Tip

❋ Many babies will take the pumpkin to their mouths to explore. Play this game after lunch when they are not hungry, and also not in the high chair used for mealtimes!

Watch, listen, reflect

👁 Watch how the baby is responding to each new experience. Look at the different ways they are exploring the pumpkin.

👁 How are they communicating with you? Watch body language as well as looking for non-verbal clues and listening to the sounds made.

👁 Look to see if the baby is imitating your actions.

Working together

Parents could:

* make time for some messy play, before bath time!
* hand objects to their baby for them to feel, - spoons, when they are making dinner, wet socks when they are emptying the washing machine and so on.

Practitioners could:

* put together some simple recipe cards for parents and practitioners with play ideas for sensory play.
* share with parents their baby's response to new experiences.

Exploring and creating

What are they learning?

are they
   reaching?
   exploring?
   using senses?
   looking?
   attending?
this leads to
   * sensory play
   * investigating
   * concentrating
   * creativity

Resources for all stages of A Competent Learner

Bargain buys for mark making

Try Pound Shops and other bargain outlets for
* paintbrushes and other decorator's tools
* sponges and brushes
* plastic sheets and shower curtains
* bargain felt pens
* funnels, tubes and sieves
* containers and pots

Try DIY stores for
* paint brushes
* sand and gravel
* dust sheets
* rollers, sponge rollers
* plant saucers & trays
* builders trays

Try Charity Shops for
* kitchen tools
* old shirts for painting
* curtains for dust sheets
* containers for equipment
* baskets for treasures
* trays and tins

Always wash or sterilise things before use.

Resources

Builder's Trays and plant trays
Get these from DIY stores

Feely Bags
NES Arnold, Galt, Early Learning

Textured balls
ASCO Educational Supplies (they also supply sensory tiles and sand boxes)
tel: 0113 270 7070

Gloop

Mix cornflour with water (and colour-ing if you want). The gloop should have a thick consistency - add extra water if necessary.

Bubble Solution

Make your own bubble solution from 2 cups (500ml) washing u liquid, 6 cups (1.5L) water and tablespoons sugar. Store in an empty gallon container. Buy the best quality washing up liquid y can afford, or use bubble bath

Finger paint

Make finger paint by mixing two tablespoons of cornflour and tw tablespoons of cold water in a saucepan. Add 1 cup of water ar cook till it is as thick as custard (stirring all the time). Store in the fridge. Colour with paint or food colouring, and add perfume oils to make it smell good.

Slime

Dissolve some Lux soap flakes in wc water in a container. Add colourin if desired. Allow mixture to stand until it becomes thick, add more water if necessary. Beat the mixtu with egg beaters until fluffy.

Songs and rhymes

These songs and rhymes are suitable for developing hands, fingers, feet and fine motor skills. They are all in This Little Puffin (Penguin Books) or in The Little Book of Nursery Rhymes (Featherstone Education)

Finger songs and rhymes

Five Little Peas
Heads, Shoulders, Knees and Toes
Here are the Lady's Knives & Forks
Here is a Box
Here's The Church Here's the Steeple
Incy Wincy Spider
My Little House
One Finger, One Thumb Keep Moving
One Potato, Two Potato
Pat-a-Cake, Pat-a-Cake
Peter Hammers with One Hammer
Roly, Poly Up and Down
Round and Round the Garden
She Didn't Dance
Teddy Bear, Teddy Bear
This Little Pig Went to Market
Tommy Thumb
Two Little Dicky Birds
Wind the Bobbin

Songs to help imitation & imagination

Daddy's Taking us to the Zoo

Dingle Dangle Scarecrow
Five Currant Buns
Five Little Ducks
Five Little Men in a Flying Saucer
Five Little Monkeys
Heads, Shoulders, Knees and Toes
Here is The Beehive
Here we go Round the Mulberry Bush
Hokey Kokey
I am the Music Man
If You're Happy and You Know It
I'm a Little Teapot
In a Cottage in a Wood
In a Dark, Dark Wood
Insy Winsy Spider
I Went to visit a Farm one day
Little Peter Rabbit
Little Rabbit FouFou
Miss Polly had a Dolly
Old MacDonald had a Farm
1, 2, 3, 4, 5 Once I Caught a Fish Alive
1 Finger, 1 Thumb Keep Moving

Pat a Cake
Peter Hammers with One Hammer
Roly Poly
Round and Round the Village
Row, Row, Row Your Boat
Sandy Girl
Teddy Bear, Teddy Bear, Touch Your
Nose
The Farmer's in His Den
The Wheels on the Bus
There was a Princess Long Ago
This is the way the Lady Rides
This Old Man, He Played One
Tommy Thumb
Twinkle, Twinkle, Little Star
Two Fat Gentlemen
Two Little Dickey Birds
We Can Play on the Big Bass Drum
When Goldilocks Went
When I was One
Wind the Bobbin up

Books about Treasure Baskets

Title	Author	Publisher
* <u>Infants at Work</u>	Elinor Goldschmied	NCB (1987)
* <u>People Under Three</u>	Elinor Goldschmied& Sonia Jackson	Routledge
* <u>The Little Book of Treasure Baskets</u>	Ann Roberts	Featherstone Education

Heads up
Lookers &
Communicators

Aspect and components

Section 4

The Following section contains activities for young babies, to help build
A Healthy Child

The relevant Birth to Three Matters components are:
* **Growing and Developing**
* **Keeping Safe**
* **Making Healthy Choices**
* **Emotional Wellbeing**

Aspect and
components

Grab - and let go

Developing fine motor skills

Heads up lookers and communicators

Aspect:
A Healthy Child

Components:
Growing and developing

Reach it -
black and white patterns

What you need
* white card
* black card or paper
* scissors, glue and ribbon
* hoop or baby gym

What you do
1. Cut different shapes, such as zigzags from the black card, and glue to the white card to make black and white contrasting patterns. Make different patterns on each side of the white card.
2. Tie the cards securely to the hoop or baby gym. Lay the baby under the baby gym or suspend the hoop securely so that the cards are within easy reach.
3. Tap the cards and encourage the baby to look at and reach to pat the cards.

another idea:
* Try tiny black and white spots or a chequer board patterns.

Ready for more?
✋ Cut eyes, noses and mouths to make black and white face patterns.
✋ Add a reflective border to the cards. Help the baby hold the card with two hands.

Individual needs

- ☼ Some babies will need you to take their hand gently to the cards.
- ☼ Tape bells to the back of the card. Shake to help the baby focus and look in the direction of the sound.
- ☼ Try sitting the baby in a baby relaxer under the hoop or baby gym.

Watch, listen, reflect

- See which patterns are most appealing to the baby.
- Watch where the baby can most easily see and reach for the cards.
- Listen and copy any sounds they make.

Tiny Tip

❊ Young babies focus best on faces and objects held at about 22cm.

Working together

Parents could:

* tell practitioners which are their baby's favourite pictures or mobiles.
* try out the cards at home.

Practitioners could:

* show parents the cards and how they are being used.
* visit the library to borrow black and white pattern baby books, and look out for black and white pattern soft toys.

Grab - and let go

Developing fine motor skills

What are they learning?

are they
looking?
turning to sound?
reaching?
sharing fun?

this leads to
* grabbing
* holding

Grab - and let go

Developing fine motor skills

Heads up lookers and communicators

Aspect:
A Healthy Child

Components:
Growing and developing

Pat it! -
texture and treasure

What you need

* a shallow plastic tray
* different textured objects - crinkly paper, a woolly sock, furry glove, toothbrush, hard plastic cup, etc.

What you do

Sit on the floor opposite the baby.

1. Make a treasure tray. Place the different textured objects on the tray. Tap the objects on the tray.
2. Talk and sing to the baby. Help them to explore the objects.
3. Try rubbing the different textures firmly but gently on the backs of their hands.
4. Encourage them to reach for and pat the objects with two hands.
5. Praise the baby's efforts at reaching with words, cuddles, gentle strokes and tickles.

another idea:

* Try patting warm, damp, bubbly sponges.

Ready for more?

🖐 Put together a tray of different textured wooden objects to pat.

🖐 Offer the objects one at a time for the baby to grasp and hold.

Individual needs

- ☼ Make sure the baby is sat securely. It is hard to reach and pat objects if you are still working on your sitting balance!
- ☼ Lift each object, show it to the child, press it gently into their hands and then tap the tray as you return it for them to reach for.

Watch, listen, reflect

- 👁 Watch for any textures that the baby really likes or dislikes.
- 👁 Look to see if they are content to pat the objects or are trying to grab the objects.
- 👁 Listen to the range of sounds they are making.

Tiny Tip

❄ Stuff a small cushion or rolled up tea towel next to the baby if their highchair is too wide.

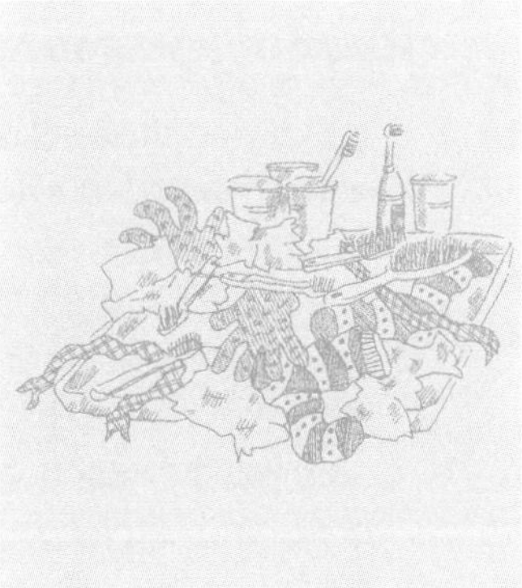

Working together

Parents could:

* bring objects from home for their baby's treasure tray.
* tell the practitioner which objects their baby likes to reach for or pat.

Practitioners could:

* share with parents the different objects their baby has enjoyed on the treasure tray.
* play together for a few moments, talking with parents about imitating the sounds the baby makes in play.

Grab - and let go

Developing fine motor skills

What are they learning?

are they
- feeling textures?
- sitting & patting?
- looking/reaching?
- showing pleasure
- exploring?

this leads to
* grasping & holding
* shaking
* letting go

Grab - and let go

Developing fine motor skills

Heads up lookers and communicators

Aspect:
A Healthy Child

Components:
Growing and developing

Grab It - sticks and shakers

What you need

* rattles
* home made or bought shakers
* small wooden spoons
* ribbons

What you do

1. Sit opposite the baby and hold the rattle out for them to reach for. Hold it in the mid line.
2. Shake it, call the baby's name and gently lift their arm from the elbow towards the rattle or shaker. Help them to grasp the rattle, shake it and share their enjoyment of the sound.
3. Tie the ribbons together in a bundle. Trail them through the baby's outstretched hands. Encourage them to grasp the ribbons, or gently twine the ribbons over both hands.
4. Offer the wooden spoon to the baby to grab and hold. Hold the spoon with them and sing 'Shake, shake, shake, tap, tap, tap'.

another idea:
* Chiffon scarves are great for reaching and grabbing.

Ready for more?

🖐 Hold the shakers to either side for the baby to practise reaching to the side.
🖐 Provide a plastic bowl full of ribbons or scarves to reach for, grab and explore.

Individual needs

☼ Some babies and children need lots of encouragement to reach and grab. Try reflective objects, such as a baby mirror. Tie bells to the mirror for further encouragement.

☼ Make sure the baby or child is sitting well supported if necessary.

Tiny Tip

❊ During everyday care, give the baby suitable objects to feel before using them, such as feeling their vest before putting it on, or holding the flannel before washing.

Watch, listen, reflect

👁 Watch which hand the baby finds easiest to reach and grab with.

👁 Watch to see if they are bringing the shaker to their mouth to explore.

👁 Watch and listen to how they express their feelings, maybe excitement, pleasure, or perhaps dislike of each object.

Working together

Parents could:

* bring in some everyday objects from home for their baby to reach for, such as a soft hairbrush, flannel, plastic spoon and so on.
* offer their baby objects from both sides.

Practitioners could:

* look out for interesting objects to encourage reaching.
* make practising reaching a part of everyday activities, such as meal times and changing times.

Grab - and let go

Developing fine motor skills

What are they learning?

are they
   reaching?
   grasping?
   exploring?
   making sounds?
   having an effect?
this leads to
   * cause & effect
   * fine motor control

Tickle and tumble

Feeling safe and supported

Heads up lookers and communicators

Aspect:
A Healthy Child

Components:
Growing and developing

Peepo -
disappear and re-appear

What you need

* a cloth, towel, blanket or sheet

What you do

1. You can play this game in many places - on the changing table or mat, in a baby chair, during feeding, or when you are having a quiet cuddle!
2. Call the baby's name to attract their attention.
3. Hold the cover up in front of your face and slowly draw it down so your face appears. Don't move too quickly with young babies, or they won't be able to follow what is happening. As your face appears, smile and speak gently.
4. Remember that very young babies may not like the 'BOO' bit to start with, so make sure you respond to their reactions and take it gently.

another idea:

* Let the baby surprise you by putting the cover very gently over their face and letting them pull it off.

Ready for more?

* As they get used to this game, most babies enjoy the predicted surprise of 'BOO' as you reappear.
* Try putting the cover right over your head and letting the baby pull it off.

Individual needs

☼ Some babies need you to start by just covering your face up to your eyes so they are sure you are still there.

☼ A baby in a stroller might enjoy being pushed away from you, then pulled back towards you with a gentle 'Boo'.

Tiny Tip

❋ Young babies focus best on faces and objects held at about 22cm/9".

Watch, listen, reflect

👁 Watch the baby's response to you, and be aware of the 'shock factor'!

👁 Watch the baby focus on your face.

👁 Look for reaching and grasping, and for kicking and other signs of pleasure.

Working together

Parents could:

* play this game with their babies in the bath or at bedtime.
* tell practitioners if their child is anxious about hiding or about loud sounds.

Practitioners could:

* talk to parents about simple games to play with their babies.
* explain how important eye contact and holding are in building confidence.

Tickle and tumble

Feeling safe and supported

What are they learning?

are they
   looking?
   turning to
   sound?
   smiling?
   sharing fun?
this leads to
   * joining in
   * remembering

Tickle and tumble

Feeling safe and supported

Heads up lookers and communicators

Aspect:
A Healthy Child

Components:
Keeping safe

106

Look at Me! - a face to face game

What you need

* no special equipment

What you do

1. Sit on the floor opposite the baby, who is seated in a chair, or against a secure and comfortable prop.
2. Make sure you are within focus distance of the baby.
3. Call the baby's name to attract their attention.
4. Sing or chant to the baby 'Here I am, here I am, close to you. Here you are, here you are, close to me'. Use the tune of 'Tommy Thumb'.
5. As you sing, stroke the baby's hand or arm.
6. Sing again 'Here I am, here I am, looking at you. Here you are, here you are, looking at me'.
7. Praise any response, such as kicking, waving, smiling, by smiling and saying 'Well done, you are looking at me!'

another idea:
* Sing the song holding the baby and looking in a mirror.

Ready for more?

🖐 Sing these little songs at changing time, or feeding time.
🖐 Use a face puppet or rattle to attract attention. Hold it near your face and move it when their attention is on you.

Individual needs

☼ Babies and small children need to feel physically secure. Make sure they are well supported wherever they are.

☼ Sing frequently to children with special needs, even when you are not next to them. The sound of your voice will be very comforting to them.

Tiny Tip

❊ Stuff a small cushion or rolled up tea towel next to the baby if their chair is too wide.

Watch, listen, reflect

👁 Look for any responses such as kicking, waving, gurgling or smiling.

👁 Watch for concentration as they listen to you singing.

👁 Note if small babies turn their heads towards you when they hear your voice, and check carefully for any child who may not be able to hear you.

Working together

Parents could:

* play very simple singing games with their babies at home.
* watch carefully for responses and tell practitioners if they are worried about their baby's responses.

Practitioners could:

* make a baby song book or put some ideas together for parents to use at home.
* model these simple games so parents can see what to do.

Tickle and tumble

Feeling safe and supported

What are they learning?

are they
    looking?
    turning to
    sound?
    reaching?
    sharing fun?

this leads to
    * grabbing
    * holding

Tickle and tumble

Feeling safe and supported

Heads up lookers and communicators

Aspect:
A Healthy Child

Components:
Keeping safe

108

Cuddle! –
feeling safe

What you need

* a fleece or baby blanket
* a soft toy or teddy (optional)

What you do

1. Hold the baby in your lap or your arms.
2. Wrap the fleece or blanket round both of you, so you are together inside the warmth. Include the teddy or soft toy if you wish.
3. Hum or talk gently to the baby, repeating their name and lullaby songs so they feel really safe.
4. Stroke their arms and hands and back. Use sounds like 'Shhh', 'Lala', 'Mmmm' and slow, gentle speech.
5. Rocking gently will increase the baby's feeling of security. *Try not to fall asleep yourself!*

another idea:

* You could walk gently around the setting with the baby in the blanket, talking in a sing song way about what you see.

Ready for more?

🖐 Sit on a bean bag or floor cushion or in a soft chair with one or two babies, just watching their world and talking gently about what you see. This will build their confidence in daily events.

Individual needs

☼ New children or those who have had difficult or stressful experiences will really benefit from this activity. Stopping and just doing this confidence building will really pay off!

☼ Some babies and children really enjoy being helped to stroke soft or furry fabrics.

Tiny Tip

�֍ Stroking soft fabrics, holding soft toys and gentle music all help children to feel secure. Areas with low lighting also help this activity.

Watch, listen, reflect

👁 Watch how the baby responds to the activity, do they enjoy it? How do you know?

👁 Watch and listen for smiles, sounds and gurgles.

👁 Note any babies who do not respond or consistently resist contact with you.

Working together

Parents could:

* spend a little time each day just holding and talking to their babies.
* relax and enjoy some cuddles at the end of the day!

Practitioners could:

* explain to parents why this activity is important in helping babies to feel secure.
* build these times into the day for each baby and child.

Tickle and tumble

Feeling safe and supported

What are they learning?

are they
    relaxing?
    watching?
    making contact?
    making sounds?

this leads to
    * confidence
    * calm
    * ability to relax

109

What can my body do?

Heads up lookers and communicators

Aspect:
A Healthy Child

Components:
Making healthy choices

110

Happy Hands -
hands together and to face

What you need
* wrist toy or elastic hair scrunchie

What you do

1. Sit opposite the baby or with the baby on your knee. Lie young babies on their back on a soft rug. Place a rolled up blanket either side of wrigglers – so they can focus on their hands rather than their escape!

2. Gently bring the babies hands together in the mid-line and sing, using a tune you are comfortable with:
   Happy hands, happy hands
   Touch it, feel it, happy hands

3. Tap the baby's hands together gently. Encourage them to feel and shake the wrist toy. Give them plenty of time for unhurried and uninterrupted exploration.

4. Sing the song again, and this time gently help the child bring their hands together in the mid-line and then up to their face so that they can gaze at their hands.

Ready for more?

🖐 Play the game with a wrist toy or bells on their ankle. Sing 'Happy Feet'.

🖐 Play lots of clapping games to encourage older babies to bring two hands together in the mid-line.

Individual needs

✿ Vary the pace or use funny voices and whispers to grab their attention.

✿ Securely attach bells to wrist toys for babies and children that need an extra reward.

✿ Look out for black and white wrist toys for added appeal.

Tiny Tip

❋ Wrist toys are a great way to encourage young babies to lie still at changing time!

Watch, listen, reflect

👁 Think about the different ways the baby is exploring the wrist toy.

👁 Watch to see if they spontaneously bring their hands towards their face.

👁 Listen to the sounds they make. How is the baby using sounds or body language to communicate?

Working together

Parents could:

* try the 'Happy Hands' song at home with their baby, perhaps as part of getting dressed, when they have put their baby's arms in sleeves and so on.

* play 'Pat a Cake' with their baby.

Practitioners could:

* make sure the words and actions of the 'Happy Hands song are available to parents.

* share with parents the importance of finger play and discovery.

Which one?

What can my body do?

What are they learning?

are they
  exploring?
  looking for the sound?
  enjoying rhymes?
  bringing hands together?
this leads to
  * clapping
  * patting
  * reaching

What can my body do?

Heads up lookers and communicators

Aspect:
A Healthy Child

Components:
Making healthy choices

112

Look and Pat -
black and white pat mats

What you need
* black and white fabric
* stick-on Velcro or a simple sewing kit
* scraps of crunchy or crinkly paper for filling

What you do
1. Make a simple bag shape using the Velcro or straight seams for the edges. Fill the bag with scraps of crunchy or crinkly paper. Seal it securely with Velcro or stitching.
2. Place the mat on a flat surface and encourage the baby to pat the mat using two hands together. Talk and sing as the baby pats the mat.
3. Copy the baby's actions and sing 'Pat, pat, pat'. Vary your voice to grab the baby's attention.
4. Try big slow movements and then quick tiny pats.

another idea:
* Fill the bag with soft sponge or feathers. Add some squeakers for added appeal.

Ready for more?
* Try patting the mat with alternate hands.
* Make a giant stamping mat with just a little filling for older or more mobile babies.
* Can older babies isolat their index finger and poke the mat?

Individual needs

☼ Add noisy toys, bells and squeakers for children with hearing impairment.

☼ Move the mat to different positions for babies and children with motor difficulties, to find the best place.

☼ Tickle backs of hands of babies with fisted hands to uncurl their fingers and pat with a flat open hand.

Tiny Tip

✽ White fabric paint on plain black fabric is a quick and easy way to transform inexpensive fabric.

Watch, listen, reflect

👁 Look to see how the child is reaching, patting and grasping.

👁 Watch and listen for how they are enjoying this play. How are they letting you know how they feel.

👁 Think about which part of the activity is most rewarding for the child and work out how you know this.

Working together

Parents could:

* put small toys on a tray for the baby to pat and explore.

* give their baby damp sponges and flannels to pat at bath time

* try the local toy library for black and white toys, pictures and patterns for their baby.

Practitioners could:

* ask parents to bring in scraps of black and white fabric and clothes.

* talk to parents about the appeal of black and white patterns to babies.

* place a black and white mobile over the changing area.

Which one?

What can my body do?

What are they learning?

are they
  reaching?
  copying?
  looking?
  using two hands
  together?
this leads to
  * exploring
  * finding out
    about bodies
  * clapping

What can my body do?

Heads up lookers and communicators

Aspect:
A Healthy Child

Components:
Making healthy choices

114

Blanket Rockers - making first choices

What you need
* a strong, soft blanket
* a soft mat, rug or mattress
* a helper

What you do
1. Fold the blanket in half for extra strength and lay it on the mat. Place the baby gently on the blanket, gather up two corners each to make a high-sided hammock.
2. Gently lift the baby in the blanket. With a soft and gentle rhythm and rocking action, sing and rock the baby,
   Rocking, rocking, to and fro,
   This is the way we go
   Rocking, rocking, to and fro,
   This is the way we stop
   Gently bring the blanket back down onto the mat.
3. Watch to see if the baby has enjoyed the activity. Offer 'Again?' Wait for some indication, a glance, a kick, a bounce, or maybe a sound to tell you that the song and rocking should be repeated.

Ready for more?
- Sing a bouncing rhyme gently jigging the blanket up and down.
- Try 'Row the Boat' and other rocking songs.
- Add 'Ready Steady Go' with a pause before 'Go', before each song or game.

Individual needs

✿ Some children with special needs find rocking very comforting and this can get in the way of them trying other things. For these children use the activity as a reward.

✿ Give lots of verbal reassurance and touches to children needing more reassurance.

Tiny Tip

✳ Roll in the sides of a small parachute to make a strong hammock for this game.

Watch, listen, reflect

👁 Look for anticipation of the song.

👁 Watch and listen to see how the child is communicating their feelings about the activity.

👁 See how they are balancing in the blanket. Are they confidently using their hands for support?

👁 Think about the different ways they are letting you know what they want.

Working together

Parents could:

* sing the rhyme as they hold their child close and rock from foot to foot.
* think about how their baby lets them know what they want.
* take a few minutes every day to sing a few simple rhymes with their child.

Practitioners could:

* make sure there are plenty of song and rhyme books available for parents to look at.
* tell parents how their child enjoyed the activity and how they 'asked' for more.

Which one?

What can my body do?

What are they learning?

are they
    enjoying new
    movements?
    asking for more?
    sharing fun?
this leads to
    * confidence
      with movement
    * finding out
      about bodies
    * making choices

115

Heads up lookers and communicators

Aspect:
A Healthy Child

Components:
Emotional wellbeing

116

Feeling Good -
baby massage

What you need
* baby oil (apricot and avocado are both good)
* changing mat
* towel, blanket or shawl

Make sure parents know what you are doing, and check for allergies.

What you do

There is a biological connection between stroking, massaging and babies growth, so try this simple hand, arm and leg massage to relax babies and reassure them.

1. Choose a warm, quiet draught-free place for this activity, but not the changing area. A quiet carpeted area is ideal.
2. Sit on the carpet or a cushion, with your back supported by a wall. Put a warm towel on your lap or the changing mat, and gently lie the baby on the towel.
3. Remove their shoes and any clothing on arms or legs.
4. Pour a little warmed oil on your hands and rub them together, talking to the baby all the time, keeping eye contact and telling them what you are doing in a quiet voice.
5. Now gently massage the baby's feet, legs, arms and hands, talking to them or singing softly all the time.
6. Use the towel to remove any excess oil when you finish.

Ready for more?
🖐 Try back or tummy massages, with gentle, soothing stroking and smoothing.
🖐 Use a shorter version of the massage just as the baby is going to sleep at rest time to help them relax.

Individual needs

☼ Gently massage the hands of children who find grasping difficult.
☼ Help children who are tense and anxious by using a gentle back massage.
☼ Babies and children who have limited mobility will enjoy being out of their chair or buggy for a gentle massage session.

Tiny Tip

❋ Keep eye contact all the time, and stop if the baby becomes anxious or wriggly.

Watch, listen, reflect

👁 Watch for massage movements that the baby likes. How do you know?
👁 Look for smiles, wriggles of pleasure.
👁 Always ask the baby if they want a massage. Get used to doing this and knowing how to respond to their non-verbal or verbal responses.

Working together

Parents could:

* try some baby massage themselves.
* tell practitioners how their baby is responding to stroking and touching.

Practitioners could:

* arrange for some baby massage sessions at the setting.
* give parents information about the links between touch and baby growth.
* offer a quiet place for parents and babies to sit at the beginning and end of sessions.

Me and you

Being together

What are they learning?

are they
  smiling?
  responding?
  enjoying massage?
  relaxing?
this leads to
  * trust
  * growth
  * confidence
  * reassurance

Heads up lookers and communicators

Aspect:
A Healthy Child

Components:
Emotional wellbeing

118

Gently, Gently -
rock and sing

What you need

* no special equipment

What you do

Rocking helps children's growth. The activity also helps with focus and eye development, as well as a feeling of wellbeing.

1. Find a quiet spot (a rocking chair, pile of cushions, settee) and sit with the baby comfortably supported in your arms.
2. Look into the baby's eyes and gently rock backwards and forwards as you sing a quiet song. Let the baby reach out and touch your face, gently stroke their cheek as you sing or hum a tune. You could sing 'Hush a Bye Baby' or 'Row the Boat', or any favourite tune in a quiet voice.

another idea:
* Have some soft music playing in the background.

Ready for more?

- Use ambient music recordings (waves, water etc.) to help with rhythm and relaxation.
- Older babies could bring a soft toy or teddy and join in the rocking and singing.

Individual needs

☼ Quiet, relaxed times are very important for children with special needs. Make sure they have quiet times frequently during the day.

☼ Children with autistic spectrum disorders may be happier rocking while they sit side by side with you. Direct eye contact may be very difficult for them.

Tiny Tip

✳ In fine weather, do this activity outside, listening to the wind, watching the clouds and the leaves.

Watch, listen, reflect

👁 Note the way children become relaxed and attentive during this sort of close relationship.

👁 Listen to them joining in with sounds and babble as they become familiar with the songs and music.

👁 Watch for children who need to withdraw and make sure they have quiet places to go, with cushions, music and low light.

Working together

Parents could:

* make sure that they have quiet times with their children.
* sing and rock with their babies.
* help their children to make a quiet place at home where they can relax.

Practitioners could:

* explain the importance of being quiet together.
* offer some tapes or CDs of ambient music, quiet songs, mobiles and night lights in the toy library or loan collection.

Me and you

Being together

What are they learning?

are they
   looking?
   listening?
   smiling?
   joining in?
this leads to
   * confidence
   * self assurance
   * relaxation
   * trust

Heads up lookers and communicators

Aspect:
A Healthy Child

Components:
Emotional wellbeing

120

Up the Arm and Down the Arm -
a singing game

What you need
* a blanket, rug or pile of cushions

What you do

1. Put the baby on the floor on a blanket or rug. If they are likely to roll away, put a cushion each side of their body.
2. Gently hold one of the baby's hands so their arm is straight. 'Walk' your other fingers up and down the baby's arm as you sing or say this song:

   Up your arm, up your arm,
   Walking up your arm.
   Down your arm, down your arm,
   Walking down your arm.

   As you reach their hand, give a little tickle.
3. Watch to see if the baby has enjoyed the game. Offer 'Again?' Wait for some indication, a glance, a kick, or maybe a sound to tell you that the song and walking should be repeated. This time do it on the other arm.

Ready for more?

- Play the same game, walking up and down legs, tummy, back. Or gently 'jump' your fingers up and down their limbs.
- Try 'Round and Round the Garden' for a change of song.

Individual needs

☼ Some children with special needs find being touched is unpleasant or frightening. Go carefully and stop if they show signs of anxiety.

☼ Let older children play this game on your arm or hand. They will enjoy the activity and it will strengthen muscles as well as strengthening relationships.

Tiny Tip

❋ Lively chanting and singing with the movements will improve brain growth and memory.

Watch, listen, reflect

👁 Watch for first and continuing signs of wanting the activity again.

👁 Note how individual children signal their pleasure and anticipation.

👁 Listen for sounds and joining in with the game, as well as wanting more!

Working together

Parents could:

* sing simple songs and make up games to use with their children at bedtime or change times.
* tell practitioners how their baby asks for 'more'.

Practitioners could:

* explain to parents how these simple games stimulate growth of bodies and brains.
* make a book of simple songs and games, and hang it on the Parents' Notice Board.

Me and you

Self awareness, identity

What are they learning?

are they
    enjoying move-
    ment songs?
    asking for more?
    joining in?
this leads to
    * memory
    * trust
    * feelings of
      wellbeing

Resources for all stages of A Healthy Child

Things to collect

Contrasting black & white toys & pictures

Photos and pictures of faces and expressions, including those of the children and adults in your setting

Pictures of situations for discussion of safety and risk

Textured fabrics

Fabrics for parachute games and swinging

Fabrics to make tents and shelters

Shawls, blankets and snuggly materials

Big sheets of fabrics to use for hiding and finding games

Hats, scarves and gloves of all types, sizes and materials

Baby clothes for big dolls

Baby items - bottles, small disposable nappies, clothes, hats, toys, toiletries

Night & day clothes for teddies & dolls

Children's safety goggles, hard hats, crash helmets

Small beds, cots or boxes and bedclothes

Bracelets and bangles

Hair brushes and scrunchies

Ribbons

Baby safety mirrors

Stickers

Bells, rattles

Flannels and sponges

Soft toys and other objects for turn taking in circle time

Cardboard boxes and tubes, all sizes and shapes

Balls of all sizes & textures

Hoops, rings and quoits

Pictures from magazines and catalogues

Torches and battery lights

Natural & everyday objects for treasure and exploration baskets

Shallow baskets and trays

Small empty containers, ice cube trays, small yogurt po

Spoons of all sizes

Straws

Paper and plastic plates

Small-world people, animals, vehicles.

Small world playground, park, street, etc

Small world and child size safety signs and notices

Road Safety signs, zebra crossings, traffic lights

Role play doctor's and dentist's kits

First aid equipment, bandages, doctors' coats

Wallpaper, wrapping paper, tissue, masking tape

Baby oil for massage (check for allergies before using nut oils)

CDs of soothing music, mobiles.

Toy telephones, (both 'mobiles' and others)

Simple tape recorder

Stories about feelings of happiness, loss, loneliness, joy expectation etc

Books and stories

Title	Author	Publisher
The Little Book of Parachute Play	Clare Beswick	Featherstone Education
The Little Book of Light & Shadow	Linda Thornton & Pat Brunton	Featherstone Education
The Little Book of Circle Time	Dawn Roper	Featherstone Education
Be Safe	The Association for Science Education from www.ase.org.uk (Safety advice for nursery and primary schools and settings)	
Road Safety Guidance	(from your local authority)	
This Little Puffin	has a whole section of baby songs and rhymes	

Collect some books about childhood fears and anxieties, and add some which emphasise security and safety.
* Fact books and stories about first experiences of visiting the dentist, the doctor, being in hospital, having a new baby, going away to stay, etc.
* Books about visits and family experiences, including celebrations, happy events, parties, etc.
* Books about families and feeling safe, bedtime and being looked after.
* Stories about night time, monsters, dinosaurs, getting lost and other frightening experiences, so children can 'practice being scared' in a safe environment.

You could ask your local librarian for suggestions of new and well loved titles - they may be prepared to lend some to your setting.

Brushes and rollers
Buy:
* decorators' brushes and rollers from DIY stores
* pastry brushes and pastry cutting rollers from cookshops
* baby hairbrushes from baby shops
* nail brushes and toothbrushes
* dishwashing and cleaning brushes from bargain shops
* craft rollers from art shops

Very small things
Try:
* hundreds and thousands and sugar strands from the cake making bit of the supermarket
* pasta stars and shapes

Cardboard tubes
Try:
* carpet shops
* fabric shops
* packing & office suppliers
* printers

For Snack Time
* plastic plates and beakers (IKEA is good value)
* small plastic jugs (check that they pour well)
* spoons for serving (look for ones with chunky handles)
* small knives for cutting fruit, bread, etc (butter knives are good)
* plastic or fabric tablecloths

	Stage 1 0-8 months	Stage 2 8-18 months	Stage 3 18-24 months	Stage 4 24-36 months
A Strong Child	Me, Myself & I; (Purple pages from: 'I Like You, You Like Me')	Being Acknowledged & Affirmed (Purple pages from: 'Look At Me')	Developing Self Assurance (Purple pages from: 'I Can Do It')	A Sense of Belonging (Purple pages from: 'Me & My World')
A Skilful Communicator	Being Together (Pink pages from: 'What I Really Want)	Finding a Voice (Pink pages from: 'What's That?)	Listening & Responding (Pink pages from: 'Let's Listen)	Making Meaning (Pink pages from: 'Get the Message)
A Competent Learner	Being Imaginative; (Green pages from: 'Touch It, Feel It)	Making Connections (Green pages from: 'Count With Me)	Representing (Green pages from: 'Make Your Mark)	Being Creative (Green pages from: 'Let's Explore)
A Healthy Child	Growing & Developing (Blue pages from: 'Grab & Let Go)	Keeping Safe (Blue pages from: 'Tickle & Tumble)	Making Healthy Choices (Blue pages from: 'Which One?)	Emotional Wellbeing (Blue pages from: 'Me & You)

All four books in this series, and the 16 original Little Baby Books, are available direct from the publisher, or from your usual book supplier. Special rates are available for bulk purchases. Please phone for details on 01858 881212